BE WISE
EVIL SPIRITS ARE REAL

By Zola Quinnen
Edited by Annette Hobday

Gilbert Deya Ministries

A TRUE STORY

ISBN -1-902571-09-6

Published by **More Than Conquerors (MTC)**
459-463 New Cross Road
New Cross, London SE14 6TA

Tel: (+ 44) 208 694 9694

Web site: www.DeyaMinistries.com
E-mail Address: gilbert@DeyaMinistries.com

Kenya Office: 4th Floor, Cargen House,
Harambee Avenue, P.O. 10796,
Nairobi, Kenya, East Africa
Tel: 00 (254) 2-253299

Author's Note

All the names used in this book are not the actual people's real names, who I had had contact with, except my husband, our daughter and some people who agreed to be identified. Should any name happen to be real, that would be a coincidence.

10% of the profit raised from the sale of this book will go to Deliverance Ministries and churches.

Unless otherwise indicated, biblical quotations are from the Authorised King James Version Bible and Good News Bible, Today's version.

Through out this book I have used the word witchdoctor, fortune-teller and herbalist to mean those men and women, who used evil supernatural powers against me for their gain.

About the author

Zola Quinnen was born in South Africa. She completed her GCSEs at Rayner, a Methodist Church Missionary school where she was confirmed as a full member in the Church and was a committed member of the Young Women Fellowship. She trained as a Primary School Teacher at Clarkebury Teacher Training College. Through part-time studies, she obtained a University Entry Certificate. Zola also holds a Secondary School Teachers' Education Certificate in English and History from Vista University in South Africa. She taught in South Africa for two years before imigrating to Namibia where she taught for eight years and was interested in the school provision of children with Special Educational Needs, in some underdeveloped communities in the country. Zola is also a graduate of Education Philosophy, specialising in Severe Learning Difficulties from Westhill College in Birmingham and a holder of Master of Education (Learning Difficulties), from The University of Birmingham. Before 30th September 1996, when Zola met the Lord Jesus Christ, she was a lukewarm Christian attending her local Methodist Church once in a while and giving a meagre contributions. At the age of 30, Zola married David, a 38 years old gentleman born in Stafford. David is from a Catholic background, but was saying he is an 'atheist' when they met. He is a graduate of Philosophy from the University of Bristol but later studied electronics, and is working as a T V/Video Engineer. He is a kind-hearted man, who never raises his voice even when he is annoyed. Zola and David were blessed with a daughter, Nicola Claire in 1992, a year after their wedding in Birmingham.

**Be Wise
Evil Spirits are Real
A true story**

dedicated to

Nicola Quinnen

CONTENTS

PART THREE

Acknowledgements.

To my husband, David, if you did not leave us for some time, we would not have seen, experienced the power of God, found the Lord Jesus, discover the truth about Satan and his agents. My grateful thanks to our daughter, Nicola, for encouraging me not to cry when the nurses were around, for being helpful and patient when I was writing this book.

I thank our family, for all their help and support when I was unable to keep our daughter, you've shared my pain:
Mr and Mrs Lang
Mr and Mrs Holding
Michael and Rita Quinnen
My mother-in-law, Mrs Dolores Quinnen

I am also very grateful to my father-in-law, Ronald Quinnen who showed his love for Nicola and I.

There are so many people who

showed love and care for our family, and they are: Pastors Elizabeth Aworolo, Elizabeth Komanya-Mthembu, Gorrohs, Amos Deya, Daniel Kavuma, Robert Kayongo, Sisters and brothers in Christ; Hannah Pieters, Ndempa Mwashekele, Eva Shikongo, Lucia Hamutenya, Lindi Mtselu, Kotsie, Mr and Mrs Luthuli, Sotha Moyo, Sibongile Jamela, Mr and Mrs Wamala, Mr and Mrs Riley and Marcelle their daughter, Venerine Ogarro, Elder and sister South, Rev. Murphy and the evangelical team under brother Chimwala and his wife, Mallys.

Some people understand that they do not deserve any acknowledgement from me, because they have already received their reward from my heavenly Father, just for caring for my family. My thanks to my publisher, Gilbert Deya Ministries, I have no words to express how this ministry has lifted me up to discover my destiny.

Foreword by Archbishop Gilbert Deya

God has given me favour through the grace of His Son of Jesus Christ in the Ministry of dealing with the devil, casting them out, destroying them and rendering them powerless by the blood of Jesus.

The book I am presenting to you, is a tool of life changing by Zola Quinnen, who went through hell because of the power of witchcraft.

She missed the grave which swallowed her enemies. I am convinced Whoever shall read this book, shall overcome witches' power and their Wickedness.

May the Glory and the Annointing of the Holy Spirit flow to whoever is going read this book in Jesus name.

Nicola's notepad

I was born on the 17th September 1992. Thank God I'm alive! I was about to die in my mother's womb when the doctors rushed me to the theatre for the operation. People know me as a cesearean baby. Since I was 4, I didn't have a dad to look up to. Years passed with nights of crying for my dad. Over this period of time, my mum took the place of my dad. God carried me through the struggle. It was very hard when I saw my mum cry. Through my mum's faith, the Lord gave her a job so that she could clothe me, feed me, look after me and comfort me, as well as getting me every day appliances that I needed. Finally, the living God who answers by fire has answered my prayer and heard my cry. My dad is coming back and I am seeing him on the 1st of June 2002.
May 2002

INTRODUCTION

The contents of this book are based on my experience. These events occured at various times, in four countries. There are witnesses to these events in these countries, because they happened publicly. This is the truth that I cannot keep to myself; I would like everybody everywhere to know that;

* Jesus Christ of Nazareth is really alive; I have seen Him move on two similar occasions, but i n different countries.

* There is power in the name of Jesus.

* Satan and his agents have less power than serious Christians who are born again and baptised in the Holy Spirit and water.

* Satan, the fallen Angel does operate realistical ly in this world.

* He uses various agents, for

example, people and demons   (evil spirits) to carry out these operations.

In my case he used my mum. I trusted my Mum. She gave birth to me, brought me up, talked to me, fed me, bought me clothes, paid my school fees, smiled at me, laughed with me, seemed to be sympathising with me and did everything which any mother would have done to her last born daughter. However, she kept a secret within herself, that she was involved in witchcraft. If God had not shown me this mystery, I would never have known that the leader to my destruction was my own mum, the woman I loved and trusted. Glory and thanks be to God, the Lord Almighty who made Jill, my relative, speak openly and publicly about her involvement in witchcraft with my mum.

This book is in **three** parts:

1. My background, influences (where I was misled from childhood to believe that ancestors have
power over our lives and that we should consult witchdoctors who protect us against evil attacks) a n d the activities of the witchdoctors.

2. It explains real events that occurred to me while I was unknowingly possessed by the demons

3. The Power in the name of Jesus and the period when demons manifested, from February 1997
until December 2001 when they were finally driven out.

This book seeks to prove that the ancestral worshipping and consultation of witchdoctors or any man, is a source of evil. It is impossible to write down everything that happened during this period because this book would be very heavy to carry.

My main aim in writing this book

is not to expose or discredit people who were, directly and indirectly involved in the evil activities which could have destroyed my entire life or glorify the Devil, but to *reveal the truth in the spiritual realm as I saw it*. The book also exposes the tricks Satan uses when attacking humankind and shows how Jesus Christ powerfully fought on my behalf when I got born again not in flesh but in Spirit. This is a living testimony.

It is similar to the Old and New Testament books in the Bible. Both the works of God and the Devil are recorded, not to glorify Satan by any means, but to teach and warn people, for example, the story of Joseph, "the dreamer." I received many revelations. People should know the truth because lack of knowledge leads to destruction. Demons are real. The demons knew that *"I was going to destroy their kingdom"* and therefore were refusing to leave my body. I do not know how they got this knowledge. For them to confess that *"I don't die because they tried to kill me several times"* is a clear indication that they are weak together with their master, Satan. They also failed to get me into worst suffering. People in the world today suffer in similar ways to myself, and this book seeks to give a solution to many similar problems, a first step is simply to say *"Lord Jesus forgive me all my sins and come into my heart."* People who are seeking for happiness and are unable to find it can use this book as a reference.

Many people can tell the balance of happiness and unhappiness in their own lives. Drawing from my experiences, it doesn't matter how much you try, how good you are, how much you care, how flexible you can be or how much you can endure, people have little control in what is happening in their lives if there are evil spirits operating against them. Accepting Jesus Christ and obeying his teachings is the only solution to these problems.

The major work in my life has been completed; I am no longer possessed by demons. They manifested while they were in my body. They also gave signs when they departed. My husband and I have reconciled. Many people who did not know or believe that demons are a reality will have a reference. God allowed this to happen to me so that people, through me, can see and learn about the Devil's tricks. I was like a book for people to read. Therefore I am able to tell about the power available when calling on the name of Jesus, and also to tell that Satan is real, and his duty is to kill, *steal and destroy* **(John 10: 10).**

This book leaves many questions unanswered because we live in flesh and the issue of the life in the spirit has not much been addressed. The law seems to have difficulty in accepting this because it finds it impossible to provide hard evidence on things that are invisible.

I do not know the reasons why all these things happened to me. In some parts of this book, I write of events that caused me to have more questions than answers about the evil spirits. My experience from being involved in this conflict has taught me that it is possible to prove the spiritual life but only if you get fully involved in it, whether to be of Jesus Christ or of Satan. This book explores both, life in flesh and in the spirit.

The tone of this book is very painful, but it is a reality. It triggers my feelings emotionally and I cannot hold back my tears, I then begin to ask many questions. Why did this happen to my family? Who killed my parents and why? Why did they die like that? Why did Jill not tell me earlier what she knew about my mother? Some of the most painful things I have to face is that my mum who caused most, if not all of my suffering and the man I loved, my father, are dead now. The police reported that they were stoned to death on the 19th June 1997 in front of their home. Their dogs ate their bodies, licked their blood until the relatives, police and TV crew arrived. The people who were suspected of killing my parents were arrested, but the stones used to crush their heads were so big that it was questionable and it was dismissed that they were the culprits. We buried my parents in the most expensive caskets on the 6th July 1997.

This is the evidence of things being put right. I have forgiven all the people who made evil contributions, whether knowingly or unknowingly, to my life and I love them too. Generally, I thought that mums love their daughters, and they wished them to be married.

When this happens they are usually delighted. However, my mum had a different view about this. Her aims were that none of her children should get married and leave the home. She wanted to be financially supported by them. She spoke about this jokingly and in my case it was revealed that she meant it.

Nevertheless, with me it didn't work out. My husband and I got married. The world was such a nice place to live in those days. Later, its cruelty was revealed. My husband tried to divorce me twice and God saved our marriage. The spirit of singleness and divorce attacked my family. My mum opened this destructive door.

I used the word 'cruelty' to indicate the pain and suffering my mum put me through by collaborating with the Devil. Some children and adults are going through similar experience in this world. In most cases the cause of conflicts is blamed on the individual. In this book I agree that people have a responsibility in their lives, but I disagree that they have total control. I had no control in what was happening to me. I was only three years old when my mum gave me away to the Commander of the Demons as his wife, instructed him never to leave me until I was dead and added to this, instructed over three thousand demons to live in my stomach. More of this is discussed in *chapter 4.*

It is unfortunate that in medical research there seems to be reluctance in distinguishing between nervous break down or neurological problems and spiritual influences. This is understandable; perhaps no one has ever had experience such as mine. I lived in the flesh and believed evidence of the flesh before, but now that I have experienced , life in the spirit I am able to talk and write about it. Experience is an excellent teacher. I am an Educational Researcher and I have good insight of human mind, but this experience has caused me to give up trusting in my intelligence but to trust my Lord, Jesus Christ.

Author, Zola Quinnen.

PART ONE

CHAPTER ONE

MY BACKGROUND

I am the eighth child in a family of nine. One of my earliest memories is from around when I was four years old. I remember bumping against the washing stand. I asked mum, "when will the day come?" I knew of the day and recognised that it was continuously dark. I wanted to know when the day would come. I was at that time physically blind. I do not know when or how I regained my sight.

My grandparents on my dad's side were rich farmers. My grandparents on my mum's side were ordinary people having enough to survive. I never saw them, although I was seven years old when my maternal grandmother died.

Along my grandparents' line there were Ministers of Religion in the Methodist church. They even wrote hymns. I was brought up in the Christian faith, the Methodist church.

My parents were both teachers. They were also successful farmers and owned two farms, which they had inherited from their parents. They tried to interest my siblings and I in farming but failed. They talked negatively of town life, and they tried to prevent us from living in the city but that also failed. Mum and Dad never had close friends and they tried to stir me in that direction, they didn't even keep close ties with other family members, cousins, uncles and aunts. They never told me the reasons for this. All I used to hear was "friends are bad". Should they have told me this, surely I would have been wiser.

My dad used to say it is a waste of money to educate girls, because they would marry and they leave their parents, and give the money they have worked for to their husbands. He also believed that it was not wise to give his daughters a higher education than his own, because they would make deals in front of him, which he would never understand, then he would laugh. Dad always said that if I wanted to further my education, I must do it at our own expense (which is what I did).

MY PARENTS

The woman who gave birth to me, my mum

My mum was a very strong influence in our family; my dad did most of the things she wanted even though he did not fully agree. She was qualified as a teacher in those days but gave up her profession when she got married, to work and supervise farm activities, while my dad was the head teacher in different Primary schools.

As a supervisor of farm workers, she had to employ people to do different tasks. The neighbours called her Ma'am, because she was a married female teacher.

Now that I know about human rights, I realise that she had no respect for human dignity. Workers never lasted long, she shouted at them and sometimes hit them, she paid them very low wages and sometimes they had to leave with nothing.

My mum also tried to foster children, but they left quickly. I remember I had to intervene to defend them sometimes. She was very hard-hearted and always in conflict with people. She never liked my dad's relatives and warned me to keep away from them. She said very strange things about them that we did not understand. For example, she claimed that Sean told her that he was given potatoes by them, and his life was never normal again.

I heard her several times expressing how pleased she was that her daughters were unmarried and therefore were supporting her. She referred to the modern furniture that was in the family home, which was bought by the youngest four girls, (including myself). I questioned her lack of concern about us getting married, and confronted her. She dismissed the matter and avoided discussion around this topic. This hurt me very much. She said bad things about Jill, even calling her a witch. It later emerged that they were in one witchcraft team.

My mum claimed to be a Christian, whether she was one or not, only God knows. She worshipped at the Methodist church first, then we moved to another church. Now I can remember how she used to criticise the Evangelist of that church who was very spiritual and she succeeded in organising a petition against him which resulted in him being transferred. The church closed down soon afterwards. She then moved to the Methodist church until her death, where she was one of the leaders in the women's group. However, at my parents' funeral these women refused to acknowledge her works of service to the church.

We had family prayers every evening. I can still remember when it was my mum's turn to pray I would fall asleep and wake up again and she would still be praying. I remember some of her words *"God allow us to enter your heaven when we are dead."* Whether she made it or not, only God knows. As a child, I used to be upset because I would be woken up for prayers when I was sleeping.

My dad, he cared for me.

Early in the morning I used to hear my dad praying. He was a quiet man when he was not provoked but he shouted loudly when he was annoyed. He did not like it when our neighbours' livestock jumped the fence to feed on our farm, he used to impound them and they had to pay a fine or he would drive them to an official camp in town, seven miles away from our farm. He also did not like it when neighbours stole firewood. He used to catch them and make them to leave the firewood at home. He did not like it when he was asked to give money, for food or to buy clothes for us. We had very limited clothing mainly seconds from the Roman Catholic Church. I only got new clothes at Christmas. My mum made them with her sewing machine. Oh I hated this!

Dad joined the South African

police force for a few years, before he went on to train as a teacher. When I was born, he was already promoted to headship in a primary school nearer to our farm.

My dad always kept dried fruit and polony in his wardrobe and would eat it alone. He taught in schools far from home most of the time and came home at weekends. He was very good at music, his choir always won in music competitions. He was respected for speaking very good Oxford English. He never had a car because he believed that it was a waste of money. I remember him talking to me looking at my car later on and saying, "we never thought we Africans could own cars, cars were driven by Europeans only." (and he would laugh)

He had a trunk, which he locked all the time. He never shared financial matters with my mother. Tim and I planned, broke in and stole some of his money. I believe that the evil spirits were influencing us to steal from him. When he noticed it he complained to my mum who defended us and shouted at him. Later in life he had a large cancerous tumour on the side of his face, he was admitted to Cape Town hospital, it was here that he became born again.

Some of my relatives that are worth mentioning in this book because of their contribution in my life are Tim, Rachel and Bev. As stated earlier these are not their real names. They have had contact with me in some ways.

Rachel liked me! She was known for being naughty when she was in her teens. She was a very outgoing person and began to drink wine with her friends, "just to socialise", she said. But later she became a heavy drinker and our other relatives did not seem to like her.

We were always together doing the

hard jobs like milking the cows, working in the fields or chopping firewood. She gave me her clothes that she didn't need. I was very close to her. I can remember an incident when she was expelled from school for fighting with a girl who said she was keeping a white rat in her trunk. She was accused of witchcraft. My mum took her back to school and hit her in front of the headmaster, then she was allowed to go back to school to continue her studies.

She tried very hard to engage in love relationships with the aim of getting married, but all was in vain. I can remember reading a letter from the mother of her fiancé who was murdered while they were preparing for their wedding. This woman was accusing her of being responsible for her son's death and of being involved in witchcraft. She did not even believe that witchcraft existed, and would often tell others, not to be superstitious.

Stories emerged, one of her friends said that he had found a man's private part in her purse. People continued to accuse her of witchraft as a result many of her love relationships broke down as she would be preparing for weddings, just like me!

She shared her goals with me. She desperately wanted to be married. Thank you Lord that you gave her a husband. She was extremely happy, and took her husband to meet the relatives. If she had known my mum's heart she would not have done so. Shortly after their return, her husband left her to go back to his mother. She applied for a divorce and it was granted on the grounds of desertion.

A few years later she remarried and gave birth to their lovely daughter. Her second husband however, was very hard on her. When she was in her mid thirties, the drinking problem had increased. She sometimes got in trouble at work. Her life became very hard and painful.

Once her husband beat her with a wire hanger. Her body, especially her back was torn and bleeding. I intervened, and couldn't understand why she was not divorcing him. At that time I didn't understand the marriage commitment. I am sorry for engaging in such 'bad' thoughts. She continued to drink heavily to such an extent that she had a bad alcohol smell. One morning she returned home having been stoned with bricks by the two sisters who were her drinking friends. Her head had been cut and was bleeding. When I asked her what had happened, she said that these women had said bad things about me, so she was defending me.

She came to me one day. She had her baby with her and was in a terrible state. The dress she was wearing was torn. I took her to her parents' home. I don't know whose suggestion it was that

I take her to a relative so that she could be "helped" by the witchdoctors. The main talk was that she should be separated from her husband, whom she loved. I did not agree or disagree to this. I left her with those people. A month later she tried to look for her husband. He assaulted her and didn't want to know her any longer. She applied for divorce and it was granted on grounds of desertion again.

She lived a miserable life trying to bring up her child alone. She wrote a letter to me, saying she was leaving the country she lived in for another country. Rachel was moving from one country to another, losing all she had accumulated just like me. In her last letter before she died she said, "don't worry, Zola, I am wise now." I never heard from her again. Rachel, I will always remember you. I mourned her death. It was very painful and I cried for weeks. I couldn't attend her funeral.

I thank my husband, David for comforting me in those difficult moments.

I was later told this story of her death;

She had a chest pain and was rushed to the hospital. On the second day, she asked for her daughter, and some neighbours brought her. She looked at her, but by that time she could not speak. On the third day she died. The post-mortem revealed a blood clot in her heart. I was devastated. I feel much better now that I know the reason for her tremendous suffering.

Good lessons can be learned from her life story. She longed for what some or most men and women desire - a happy marriage. She tried to get this by herself. Evil forces tried to prevent her from getting married. God by His mercy intervened, and was by her side. She got men who wanted to marry her, but the evil spirits of singleness and divorce attacked her. She never made Jesus the cornerstone of her home. Perhaps she didn't know, just like me! The forces of darkness succeeded to break down her home. She didn't know that there were evil forces behind the destruction of her home, just like many people today lack this knowledge. She thought it was "normal", because many people divorce anyway. She tried the second husband, the same pattern continued and still she did not question this, like many people today. She was considering moving on to husband number three when she died. Some men and women continue this pattern up to spouse, number twelve or even more. Would you call this normal?

When evil spirits are involved in destruction, pain is eminent, but many people don't know this because evil spirits are invisible. They live in human bodies. Somebody has to cause the destruction. At that time they are under the control of the spirits. There is not much they can do by themselves. If you're one of these people, be wise.

Bev happened to know all my affairs and business. She visited some of the witchdoctors I recommended to her and I also visited many others on her recommendations. I was spiritually blind that time, or shall I say I had to get involved in that venture so as to know the truth about these people, in order to warn generations to come. She did not get on with my husband at all, but I always took sides with my husband. When problems started between my husband and I, she organised a delegation to go and help us to settle the dispute and I got back my wedding ring which, I threw at him through the window. This was very kind of her!

My husband refused to let her be

involved. Only God knows the reason. I can't understand why she was accused her of being an agent of the Devil by one of the relatives. Not long after that this accuser died in a car accident, at the same time as Rachel died. They were buried one after another. My other relatives loved her, gave her clothes, kept her in the warm room with them while Rachel and I were always doing the hard work. She always claimed that my mum did not love her. (Who did she love anyway? Only God knows).

I thank her for assisting me to obtain a scholarship to read my degrees. I love her. She told me one day that it doesn't make them feel good that I'm more materially blessed than they are. She made sure that she obtained every thing she needed, except a man to marry her. She worked very hard.

Until now there are still many things that she said and did that I don't understand. Such as what she said one evening when she came to our house at midnight because "there were many lizards on the wall of her house." I can't understand why she fainted and wanted to stay in the hospital when I prayed very hard and fasted. I can't understand what she meant when she wanted us to drive behind each other when we had to attend the funeral of my parents.

I still wonder what she meant when she said, she had a feeling something was wrong and was insisting that we should drive at the same time. Why did she connect that journey with the one when they were returning Rachel's corpse for the burial? At that time the car left the road and the car owner had to use a medicine from the witchdoctors. I can't understand why she told me that I "would" suffer if I leave her.

Most of all I can't understand why I saw her in those visions. Why did the demons call her when they were burning with fire from Heaven? Why did the demons say she is keeping the keys of my mum's coffin? Why did I see the shadows running and trying to hide behind the hills, when the demons were saying she is hiding behind the mountains? Read more of this in *chapter 6.*

Tim was also very close to me. I can remember, he told me that our farm was on fire but no one was seen around to start this fire. The thatched roof house also burned down.

Something very strange happened one Sunday afternoon. We were both outside and he said to me that if he lifted a piece of corrugated iron that was on the ground there would be fire beneath it. I said, "do it." As he lifted this piece of iron the grass started burning and as I was running to call the grown ups, he threw it on the flames and with one bang all the fire stopped.

He used to have money on his underpants in the morning, a lot of notes. He gave me this money. I remember sleeping by him in bed and he sent me to call my parents. My mum went to him and told me to go away. I looked through the keyhole and listened. A voice with a tone smaller than his came out of him. My mum was talking to it. Now I know those voices were evil spirits. The voice said that they were lucky because they (meaning demons) were related to them. Therefore they would not hurt the boy. My mum was telling them to go. They would not go and said they had information concerning the whereabouts of our relatives. The voice said that they were sent to kill the boy and demanded money if they had to leave. My dad went out to put this money on the windowsill. Something was going on and my mum was behind it. Could the money Tim always found be that of my dad?

He got married but his wife left him soon after. She also told her own disturbing stories about my family. He was badly hurt and wanted her to return.

Family memories

Whenever my mum was not working I was with her. I served her and my dad with early morning tea regularly (usually 6am). She always asked me to do her hair and would fall asleep. I impressed my parents with my good schoolwork, and they always praised me. Sometimes my mum would cuddle me. She deceived me, she engineered my downfall and let me down. But I forgave her. Before she died I wrote a letter to her in reply to one asking me for money. The letter said, *"Mum, I have forgiven you. I am going to give you money."* I had already taken her account details to set up a direct debit. She also asked me to return home, this never happened, instead I moved further away.

My mum never laughed loudly but I can remember her smile. She shouted loudly when she was annoyed and arguments with my father were mostly about money. They were always in conflict with neighbours about livestock and water.

My first attacks in life

In 1977 I met a man through a friend. I did not allow him to have sex with me but he overpowered me. I had gone to his place with my friend and he promised that we were not going to stay long. He invited me to his bedroom, but I never for one moment suspected that he would force me into it. If it were today I would have opened a rape case against him.

Three months later I discovered that I was pregnant. I can still remember the pain when I told him that I was pregnant with his child. He told me he was on a pill that made him infertile, so I must find the man who had really made me pregnant. What a blow! I cried and felt very lonely and scared, but I had to find the courage to face my parents. I left the college where I was training to be a primary school teacher and returned home. When I told Mum she was extremely upset and hit me very hard with a stick. He turned out to be a distant cousin of mine. I could not cry, I just said, "sorry Mum."

Eventually my parents stopped shouting at me after they had gone to his parents and he had admitted responsibility. They came to a financial arrangement and he agreed to pay the money my parents demanded in instalments. His family wanted to discuss arrangements for after the baby was born, but my mum refused. She actually said, "they must just pay and then go away." I loved him and wanted us to get married. Now I know the reason for her refusal. She knew that she had given me away to the commander of demons, she could not contradict herself.

When I was about eight months pregnant my mum told me that she had met him and he was being escorted to the mental hospital. She said that he was mentally disturbed, and that I should forget about him. She said that he might even be very dangerous. I never saw him again and he never contacted me. Oh I was hurt! I needed him.

At this time I went to live with another relative. A man in this home wanted to abuse me sexually through deceit. I only told my mum, as I did not want to jeopardise his marriage. I attended antenatal clinic regularly and everything was all right. The last attendance before delivery was Thursday and everything was fine.

Next Monday morning, I felt labour pains, and walked to the hospital. The nurse told me that the baby was not moving. I gave birth to stillborn child. During delivery the placenta came first, however there was no other explanation given from the hospital as to why my baby died, they just disposed of the corpse. I did not mind or feel hurt; at the time I was not ready to be a mum. My mum phoned the next day to ask about the baby, when I told her that he was dead, her reaction was just "ooh" in a low voice. She refused to inform the man's family.

But how did a witchdoctor, who lived 600 km from my family, know about the incident? About 18 years later she told me during a consultation, that the baby had not been buried properly. She said he was causing bad luck for me; therefore I had to build a house for the ancestors and to call his soul to rest. Is there a connection between witches and witchdoctors? So who is fooling whom? I know I fell into the Devil's trap!

God kept me away from mum.

The following year I returned to college. I still loved this man and I tried to make up with him, but he did not want to know. The spirit of rejection was at work in my life. Many times I was hurt. I never wanted to change men like underwear; my mum had led me into a trap.

I was 19 years old when I started teaching at a village very far away from my home. My mum did not want me to go there, but Dad supported me. He hired a car and drove me to the village.

This was something he had never done for any of his children. *I still do not know why my dad had to die such a terrible death.*

People living in my new place of work were of a different tribe. They spoke a different dialect and I accepted this appointment happily. I seldom visited the family farm, but whenever I did, I gave my mum money. From my first salary I bought them a dining room suite which was very expensive at the time. I also bought my mum a pair of shoes. I always spoke to my dad on these visits, but I feel I should have related more to my mother, as I was a girl. We spoke about things in general, but never discussed subjects such as love affairs in depth. Whenever I tried to engage her in this topic, her answer was, "it is better not to be married."

I began to get involved in love relationships with the aim of finding my future partner. Little did I know that what was in my mum's heart would continue to affect my life, even miles from home. Many men fell in love with me, but they just left me for no reason. I tried very hard to love, seeking to be loved in return. I can remember how I used to cry and let go. The demons were in my body, fighting me from within. The demon commander did not allow any man to be around me for a long period. It hurt me deeply. It didn't matter who I met and fell in love with, nothing worked well for me, and the spirit of rejection stalked me.

I remember taking the man who wanted to marry me home, as this was the custom. He paid 10 pounds part dowry, which was meant to confirm that he wanted to marry me. A few weeks after our return he was caught in a compromising position with a schoolgirl, I witnessed them being taken to the head tribesman. I ended the relationship. We were both in tears, he was crying for me not to leave him and I was crying because I felt used and betrayed. It hurt me very much. The engagement was over but my mum refused to refund the dowry money.

She was very happy to receive the money while knowing very well that according to her she had already given me a spiritual husband, therefore it was hard for me to get married. It took the mercy of God from heaven that I got married at all. Thank You Jesus! My mum loved money, she answered in a vision that she did all this evil for money. The love of money is the source of all kinds of evil.

Readers, have you been trying to get married? Now it's time for you to rise up and find out the truth through Jesus! Demons are assigned to carry out their duties to kill, to steal marriages and to destroy happiness. *(Read chapter 4)*

They accused me of being evil

I left the country where I was born and went to Namibia. Not many people knew me there. Men fell in love me and I tried to engage into love relationships, but the same thing happened again and again, they just dropped me like a bag of potatoes. Joe was one man I fell in love with; he did the same thing to me. I later discovered that his reasons for leaving me were very sinister. One day he decided to come back to me, I asked him why he had left me. He said that I was the talk of the city. He said that he feared for his life, he was warned to be careful because my boyfriends always died.

I told him that I'd never killed anyone; I didn't even know how to kill. I began to recover from the pain of being rejected by him, but I desired revenge. So, I agreed to engage into a relationship with him again, and this caused conflict between him and another girl he was seeing. One evening he came to collect me to spend the night at his place, I told him, "I will rather sleep with a dog than with you." He hit me, we got into a fight, and a neighbour heard me screaming and came to my rescue. This relationship was closely followed by other relationships that didn't work. Life did not seem worth living.

I hated African men, I tried to forget about them for sometime and I worked day and night at the same time. But I was very lonely. I spent weekends alone in the house with no one to speak to. Not even the phone would ring. I would end up singing to distract the silence. I tried to be in love again and have relationships, because of loneliness, but it just didn't work out and I did not understand why. Friends and colleagues advised me to go to witchdoctors and fortune-tellers to find out what was going on. This was the beginning of my involvement with them. I write about this in *chapter 2*. The pain from the constant rejection became unbearable. I was heading down a very dangerous pathway. My mum, the woman I loved, had caused this pain. But…what made her to take this decision?

I can still remember, following this I was fornicating for three years, not knowing that this was wrong. At this time I had no idea that it was *against God's laws to have a sexual relationship with a man you are not married to.* He had promised to marry me and I had hoped that we would have a family together. We never quarrelled or differed in opinions. One day, he too, dropped me just like that. He said he just didn't want me. What had I done to deserve this? I was faithful in every relationship, I always provided the most, in cash and in kind. He just didn't want to know. I was deeply hurt. I just did not understand. At this time I had knowledge about suicide. I carried all I needed, as I visited him to plead for one last time. But it was over. He despised and insulted me. He said, "Go away, I don't want you, you are sticky, and you name it." I gave up, nothing worked, and I did not attempt suicide. The Lord protected me for a good reason - to be one of His Servants.

I gave up on relationships. I did not want men. I hated them! Years passed by, I was happy on my own, although I sometimes felt very lonely. The spirit of singleness continued to attack me. I made up my mind, never to be involved with men with the same colour skin as my own; they hurt me, and were ungrateful. In fact when God revealed the truth which this book is all about, I realised that it had nothing to do with the colour of the skin. I did not know that the demon commander was chasing them away. This is exactly what my mum wanted.

The suicide thoughts

I met another man who was known in the community I lived in. He was going to leave and I felt I could not face another scandal. I thought of something that could finish me, thus relieving the mental and emotional pain I was feeling. Life was no longer worth living. I reached the point where I could not take the pain of rejection anymore. The spirits of death and hell were actively operating in me. All I was hearing was "die you will never feel hurt again. You will never be rejected again." Those were the lies of Satan. Many people have died in similar way. Only those who are left remain with unanswered questions as to why they committed suicide. Because they can't tell, others draw conclusions that they chose to die.

After a long time on my own I met and fell in love with another man. He had just been divorced by his wife and was looking for love. I did not know the pain of marital problems, especially when only one person wants to end the marriage. Forgive me Lord for falling into that trap of Satan. I thought I had met the right person, he had respect for human beings and he did not want to hurt anyone. As I did not believe in relationships with no future, we discussed marriage and I thought we were both sure of what we each wanted.

I took him to my home to introduce him to my parents. A week later, after our return to Namibia, our relationship ended, he finished it. We both cried as we were parting. I left the house we were sharing. I again chose to be on my own, without any man. My love for God began to grow stronger. I met a man who also loved God, and we became friends. He was not married, I liked him, but I had made a decision never to be involved with men again. I was wrong I did not know that my husband was on the way.

My tears changed to happiness.

I decided to pursue my career hoping that I would find happiness and fulfilment in my work and forget about marriage. God opened my way to England and this was the beginning of my temporary relief from the spiritual forces that had been blighting my life until then. I was separated from my family. I had no contact with my parents. Was this the plan of God? I believe it was. God can make a way where there is none! He did this for me, therefore He can do it for anyone.

I met the man who was to become my husband. We were both very happy

Zola's Wedding to David in December 1991

because we had found each other. We felt that we were a gift for one another and we got married. None of my family or friends from home knew about the wedding, only God knows why I did not inform them. I thank Him now, glory be to you Lord Jesus, forever. Our wedding was on the 14th December 1991. My dream came true. I walked down the aisle hand in hand with, my husband.

The demon commander was still in my stomach, but because God Almighty had said, "yes" no person or anything could say "no". A year later, our beloved daughter was born. My happiness was complete.

If I had known my mum's heart, I would not have sent her our wedding photo. If I had known my mum's heart I would not have taken my husband home to meet my family. If I had known God then, as I know him now, I would have heard Him warning me not to go. If I had known that some of my family members were involved in witchcraft, I would have sought the Lord Jesus Christ to ensure protection, surely I would never have got involved with the evil that nearly destroyed me.

Why did the Lord not protect me? He allowed Lazarus to die. Jesus did not go when He was called. He waited for four days until Lazarus was buried. He raised him from death in order for His name to be glorified **(John 11; 1-27)**. God allowed all the suffering to happen to me so that I would come to Him and see His power.

CHAPTER TWO

I CONSULTED WITCHDOCTORS AND THIS IS WHAT THEY DID TO ME

It may seem odd to reveal the practises I engaged into unknowingly. I am not ashamed to write about them. God has forgiven me and has kept no record of all the ungodly things I did. This is just like He did to King David who set a trap for Bathsheba's husband to be killed because he wanted her to be his wife **(2 Samuel 11:27)**. The story was recorded not to promote any evil but to teach the lost. I know that there are people who are having their lives like I've had. They are seeking help from fortune-tellers, spending lots of money which they could use for themselves. They are not aware of this network, which is there to destroy them and inflict more pain. Some body somewhere, has to come out and speak about the truth they have seen and experienced in order for the others to know that there is God, who is saying even today. *"Come to me all of you who are tired from carrying heavy loads, and I will give you rest."* (**Matthew 11:28**)

When I heard this promise, I believed it, therefore I am bold enough to come out and write about the wickedness of the Devil and the reality of the Lord Jesus Christ. He is the way to solve all problems. His help is free! Jesus has already paid the price with his blood. Therefore we do not pay the powerful men and women of God, who drive out the evil spirits in the name of Jesus. If you have ears, hear what the Spirit of God is saying to you!

What are witchdoctors?

Why are they called witchdoctors? By whose power do they operate? Are they there to help or to destroy? I have never thought of finding out how this word witchdoctor was invented. Neither have I ever thought of proving their activities. Until today after I have fasted and prayed, seeking the Lord to have the courage to look into the trap that I unknowingly fell into.

The Oxford dictionary describes a witchdoctor as a male tribal magician (especially among primitive people). A witch is described as a woman said to use magic especially for evil purposes. The Oxford dictionary gives the following explanation for magic: "Magic is art of controlling events by the pretended use of supernatural forces/witchcraft." I looked for the meaning of evil in the same dictionary and it gives these adjectives, wicked, sinful, bad, harmful...and quotes the evil one, the Devil. The Devil is Satan the fallen angel. Does satan exist? He does, and I have witnessed his evil schemes and attacks in my own and in my loved ones lives.

Some people say they do not believe that Satan exists. This is one of the strategies the Devil is using to attack people, especially those people who say he does not exist. He uses the evil spirits of unbelief to take control of them, then begins to attack different areas of their lives. These people normally say they don't believe in anything, but some if not all their actions reveal the works of Satan. These people are not seeking protection from the Lord; they do not realise that they have an enemy who is seeking to destroy them. Reader, if you are one of these people you have to act quickly, you need to know the truth about God.

The Bible says that the Devil

exists, *"Whoever continues to sin belongs to the Devil, because the devil has sinned from the very beginning. The Son of God appeared for this very reason, to destroy what the Devil has done."* **(Good News Bible 1 John 3: 8)** When the Bible says so, who can deny this truth? The Devil's instruments for this evil were the witchdoctors.

These people were men and women, young and old. Some, but not all, of the women were married, but all the men were married. I visited them in various countries. Some of those I visited claimed that; "they had ancestral spirits in them, and these spirits gave them information when they were examining me, and were also advising them of which medicines to give me."

They wore beads around their necks or wrists, some wore ordinary clothes and seemed quite normal. I visited one of their graduation ceremonies where girls as young as 15 were recruited and trained to be witchdoctors. These are some of the memories that I pray the Lord will completely erase from my mind. I was advised by my relatives and my friends to consult witch doctors. Unfortunately I followed this advice and became involved with them. These people used trickery and lies to get me to trust them.

I was a "lukewarm" Christian, going to church once or twice a month; I did not know the God I served. I was blind, I had my Bible, but I did not know it. Thank you Jesus for sending a sister to tell me about the peace you can receive, "when you give your heart to Jesus." After all the experience I have had with these evil people, I have so many questions of which many are now being answered. I had to be in the same boat with Jesus. **(Read chapter 4)**

These people lied and said that God was helping them because the herbs they were using came from the trees that He created. I deeply regret and repent of my involvement with them, and I thank my Lord Jesus Christ for his wonderful forgiveness and for not keeping a record of the wrongs I did under their instruction. I needed help; sadly, I sought it from the wrong people.

Why did I turn to them for help?

I knew for a long time that something was not right with me. I knew that my life was not normal. I knew that somebody had made my life very difficult, very painful, and very hard, the tears I shed could perhaps have filled 50-litre container. Day and night I had no peace. I felt the pain inside my chest. I was attacked in the area that most women long for, a husband and a happy family. Little did

I realise that these evil people already had a hold in my life, reaching right back into my early childhood.

Already I had survived death through car accidents, three serious ones and two minor. Many times my mind registered that life was not worth living. Yes, death was surrounding me, but it just did not happen. My mum although for some time I did not realise the power that she held and the witchdoctors had a great deal of access to my life, they even had the opportunity to directly kill me. What stopped them from doing so?

They had access to my life but not to my soul, the Lord refused to give them that! I never stopped talking about my misfortunes. People who were all older and (I thought) wiser than me, encouraged me to consult the witch doctors. They all used these people for "help" with their own problems. I disobeyed God by seeking answers from the witchdoctors.

What they did to me.

They physically, emotionally, sexually and financially abused me. They promised to bring a change for the better in my life, something impossible for them to do. They kept me waiting for this better life, only for me to find that I was actually heading for my death. Twice I refused to get involved with them, but this became impossible as I was controlled by evil practices even before I had any control over my decisions. My mum, the woman I loved and trusted made a covenant for me when I was three years old.

Physical abuse at the age of eight

I now remember that when I was about eight, a man used to come to my home in the early evening. I would be called into the room. My mum would not give a long explanation; she would simply say that I needed protection from the evil (dirty) things.

This man used a razor blade to make small cuts in different parts of my body, head, breast, arms and both legs (these marks are still visible). A black stuff, called medicine would be rubbed into these bleeding cuts. I never cried. I would be quiet until he'd finished. This used to hurt afterwards. I remember a medicine, that shon in the dark but it was smoky when you applied it. My mum used to smear my body with it. She claimed to be protecting me. When this man had finished and had left we would all gather for evening prayers, say the Lord's prayer and either mum or dad would finish the prayer by saying, "I ask these things in the name of Jesus. Amen." We would then go to sleep. This practice continued until I was 18 years old. Did my parents know what this practice was leading to or they were cheated themselves?

Emotional abuse from the age of nineteen

My mum never bothered with protection after I reached the age of 19 and left home to begin my career. I went to teach in a village far away from my home. I discovered that the people in the village lived a very primitive life style. They practised the ancestral worship and belief publicly; in fact the headman was a witchdoctor. They held their meetings regularly and it was easy to know the house they were in because of their singing and beating of the drums. I tried to settle down in this village, but it didn't work out, the evil spirits continued to operate in my life. It was at this time that my fiancé was discovered with a schoolgirl, and the string of painful and disastrous love affairs followed.

After two years I left that village to live in Namibia, where I met other tribes who were very strong in their ancestral beliefs. It was at this time that I was encouraged to seek the help of witchdoctors. In all these cases, somebody was always available to take me to them. When I told this Christian lady about misfortunes, she encouraged me to go and look at what was troubling me. She was much older and more experienced than I. She was also a very committed believer and I trusted her judgement.

When I went and consulted the witchdoctors, I always asked her to go in with me and listen, so that I did not misinterpret the information given to me. Different witchdoctors used different approaches of examination. I visited so many and I can not write about all of them. Mainly this is what happened on each visit. The witchdoctors would have different rituals and methods of invoking their "ancestral spirits" to give them information. For example, some would have a bag with bones, dice, playing cards and dominoes. I was once told to blow into the bag then I was given the bones to hold and scatter, I was then spoken to about matters relating to my life by the "readings" of the scattered bones.

Different ones used different methods, many of which are too horrendous to write about, but needless to say, I went through many degrading and painful rituals in the pursuit of truth and peace.

Most of the witchdoctors told me

things from my past that were correct. They also told me that my enemy was from my own family. I still did not understand this at the time. I know that I disobeyed God. Yes, people perish because of lack of knowledge.

God says in His Word clearly:

"Do not go for advice to people who consult the spirits of the dead. If you do, you will be ritually unclean." **(Leviticus 19:31)**

The scriptures continue: *"If anyone goes for advice to people who consult the spirits of the dead, I will turn against him and will no longer consider him one of my people."* **(Leviticus 20:6)**

I fell out of the Glory of God. It is hardly surprising that my situation was getting worse.

Before every consultation I had to pay whatever amount of money they asked for. I switched from one witchdoctor to another, because they were not helping me. The problems I encountered became more and more serious. I was so stupid, that I continued taking their advice although I was convinced that they were not helping me. I was unable to make my own decision. I had no control of what was going on around me. In fact witchdoctors do not help anyone. It was after these consultations that they told me the ancestors were complaining. I had to return home and make a feast, slaughter a sheep and make a traditional beer for them to acknowledge their existence. Now I know that that was blood sacrifice, and idol worship. God prohibits this **(Leviticus 19:4).**

I managed to buy a new car. One of my aunts advised me to take it to a witchdoctor for protection. This lady also instructed me to do the ceremony and introduce the car to the ancestors, so that they can protect me from evil. I did everything they told me to do. This is the car that overturned on the way from home. When I confronted her afterwards, she lied and said; "if it was not protected you would have died." That accident left me with witchcraft stigma. I was the talk of the city. People said that I had killed the man who was driving at the time of the accident. I could not understand how they could say this; I was in the same accident. The full accident report is given from page later in the book.

I just couldn't see the reason or understand this pattern of destruction. The pain was too much! The witchdoctors charged me a lot of money for consultation and treatment so I lost a large amount of money through my dealings with them.

I later bought another new car, I took it to the witchdoctor. I survived two serious accidents in that one. By the grace of God, I summoned the strength of will to refuse to put any medicine in my cars after this and consequently I never had any car accidents again. I have a good reason to declare war against those who are not doing the will of God. They should repent or perish.

Sexual Abuse

I was introduced to another male a witchdoctor whom I was to consult about ridding myself of the terrible "bad luck" I was having. He said he needed male sperm to mix with the medicine. He then sexually abused me. I was disgusted and hurt by this, but I couldn't cry. He said that was the only cure available to enable a man I was in love with, to return to me. However, he never wanted to see me again.

Another male witchdoctor told me to come to his house at two am because the medicine that would help me had to be applied in the graveyard. He directed me to a cemetery, and he too sexually abused me. Why did I agree to this? My free will was surpressed. Why did I have contact with the dead? What has the dead got to do with the living? It wasn't long after that my ex-fiancé died in a bomb blast. No one could question this because it happened in a war zone. He had already finished with me before his death. At one stage we discussed marriage. It never worked out. One may wonder why do I write about these witchdoctors? The answer is simple, there are many people out there who are still fooled by these people. This is a good warning.

Someone has to expose these evil practices so that others can be saved.

Physical abuse

All of the witchdoctors that I consulted gave me medicines that I had to drink and vomit. Others I had to burn in the house. Some I had to wash and bathe in. Mostly they cut my body with razor blades.

I consulted another witchdoctor, who told me about the stillbirth that I had had about seventeen years previously. The hospital might have disposed of the body. I was amazed that she knew about my past, because she lived far away from my family. She told me that the baby's soul was not at rest, She said he wanted to be returned home and given a formal burial. She told me that I had to build a house for the ancestors. Again my life was linked to the dead.

I went home and told my parents. I bought cement and building materials. With two other women I built that house in three days. It was very hot, and I had to dig holes for the poles. My mum was watching us. She prepared food for us. She did not seem very interested in what we were doing, but she did not discourage us. She had no sympathy at all for what I was enduring, but she claimed to love me!

So I actually built a house for the demons. Read about the end of this house in chapter 5. At this time, two pairs of my knickers disappeared from the clothesline. I found them both a day later. Where did they go? Who made a knot in the red ones? Why did I not get them at the end? One of my family members suggested that she should take them to the witchdoctors to look at? I never got them back again. Here below I explain another incident of physical abuse.

I have lived with it and never had the opportunity to tell what happened as I saw it. However, I was accused of "killing". No one has ever given me the opportunity to explain my own version of what happened one Sunday morning.

In December of the previous year I intended to drive my car home to show my parents. As I was a new driver and the distance was long I offered a lift to some guys who I knew from primary school, so that they could share the driving. We had a nice journey home and we gathered together for some Christmas celebrations.

When the holiday was over and we had to return, we left on the Saturday evening at 6pm. One of the guys, was taking his fiancé, back with him. Both men occupied the front seats and the lady and myself were sleeping in the back. We reached the town near to the borders of South Africa and Namibia at about 7.00 am the following morning. We stopped at the petrol station. It was on a Sunday morning... I can still remember.

I volunteered to drive, so I moved to the driver's seat but one of the men wanted to drive, so I moved to the passenger front seat. The lady and the other man, who had been driving overnight were sitting at the back. As we set off, I noticed that he was driving extremely fast. I told him to slow down as we did not want to die. He assured me that everything was under control. After a few more metres he began increasing speed again, no one was talking.

I noticed that the car was driving to the other side of the road. With my right hand I turned the steering wheel back to the road calling to him. The car drove forward on the road. I can remember seeing big oval shaped eyes and two hands holding the steering wheel. I thought it was him, but the demon later confessed to driving the car, just before the accident. I heard a loud bang and I could not remember anything else until four days later.

My first recollection from that time is being pushed in a wheel chair past a mirror. My face was very badly swollen, my hair infront was cut and I had stitches in my head, my left arm was in a plaster and had to be examined by the doctor. My family came to see me and I remember I was talking about my work. Every time I asked a question they told me everything was fine and everybody was fine. Rachel also came to see me.

They asked for me to be discharged from hospital and I was flown back to Namibia. During the flight I heard somebody asking Rachel about the accident and whether I was driving the car. She said, "the driver died on the spot." I asked her where the man was, and she said she had been lying to the person on the flight in order to gain her sympathy.

However it was true, the man had

died. The post-mortem revealed the cause of death as swallowing his tongue. He was held by the seat belts, but the body was outside as the car overturned three times. I flew out of the windscreen as the car was overturning for the second time and fell on the side of the road. Our friends who were driving behind us had witnessed the accident and this was their version of the events. Our car was driving well above the speed limit.They noticed the car driving off towards big rocks that were along the road. It returned to the road then began to overturn. So when I turned the steering wheel I actually prevented the car from crashing into the rocks. Now I know God was watching us.

I was driven to one of my aunties' house and because I could not walk, she sent us to the hospital. My injuries were extensive, the x-ray showed a broken pelvis, which is why I couldn't walk. I broke two of my teeth and had to wear dentures for seventeen years. Dentures at the age of 24! What implications did they have? Think for yourself… Thank you Jesus that you have healed my body and made it possible for me to have tooth implants.

Four thousand pounds was worth spending for them. What a draw back? I had many injuries, I had been in a coma for four days. I had to lie still on my back for more than six weeks. I couldn't do anything for myself. I was washed and fed by people. Someone had to bring and empty a bed pan for me. Thank you "cousy", for stepping in when nurses were tired of helping me to toilet in bed, perhaps it was too much for them. Many people who saw me that time cannot believe when they see me now, wearing high heeled shoes! Thank you Lord.

When I was in the hospital. I can remember one morning, not a normal visiting time, I was sleeping. I felt something like spiders' web. As I wiped it my hand made contact with another. It was my mum's hand. She was smearing me with a black liquid which was very smelly. One of my relatives who was with her wiped me with a flannel and told her off.

They did not sit there for long before they left. What was she up to? Why didn't she speak to me? Why didn't she give me some fruit or flowers? What was her aim of smearing me with that liquid? One may wonder why didn't I ask these questions while my mum was alive. At that time I thought it was a normal car accident. Only after the revelations I got, that I realised, it was a spiritual affair made by MAN.

Now I assume that man didn't have to die in my car. Had I known of my mum's activities, I would even have kept away from other people. I would have left the country long before then. He was a bread winner in his family. Now I understand why they accused me of killing him, although I am not the culprit. My mum was responsible. She had decided to kill me, but God protected me, although I was not born again then. Thank you Jesus for your mercy!

My fiancé had disappeared

When I was discharged from hospital I arrived home to face another disaster. My fiancé who I had left to look after my flat while I was away, had disappeared. In a newspaper there was an article about a man who had left a note before committing suicide. I looked at the note and I recognised the hand writing as that of my fiancé. This is what it said;

*"If found the state may bury my body.
I found that my body deserves a
pauper's funeral."*

He left another note for me.
*"Zola forgive me, the burden was too
much to abide.
Yours forever."*

The late Reverend, from the
Methodist church where I belonged
confirmed the news of my fiancé's
death to me. He explained that it had
nothing to do with me according to the
note, but by that time I was the talk of
the town. I was accused of killing these
two men. I heard these dreadful
rumours and I was very hurt. I chose
not to have contact with anybody. I was
alone most of the time.

Of course the car in which the
accident happened was written off and
the insurance paid. I bought another
new car. Not long after that I was hit

Zola before her wedding. No one could tell that she was demon possessed.

Zola and David making their vows before God and other witnesses - never to leave each other.

Zola smiling because she had found a faithful husband

Nicola after her
5th Birthday

Nicola after her
10th Birthday

Zola's Wedding to David in December 1991

from the back. A few months later I had another accident when a car from a side road did not stop at the stop sign and drove into the front passenger's side of my car. I survived but the car was badly damaged.

A few years after that I had yet another nasty accident. It was about 7am I was driving with two passengers. It was a gravel road so I was driving at 60kmph. The car seemed to be swerving with the back wheels. I felt the car going up and I screamed. The car rolled over the bonnet and landed on its roof. No one was hurt, but the windscreen fell out and the roof was damaged. That was the last car I took to the witchdoctors. I've had three cars since then and none of them has ever even been broken down.

Sometimes I had to endure discomfort

A few years later, I drove for twenty four hours to consult a herbalist again with our daughter. We lived in the single quarters of this mine, where he was residing. It was very dirty. We slept on the floor. I had to get up early in the morning and vomit with five litres of medicine. The steaming was worse, when red bricks were put in the water. A group of other people or patients were covered in the small hut for this steaming process. He cut my body very deep and I bled. He took me to the bush and made a fire. I had to vomit over that fire. He took me to a river, while those cuts were still bleeding. I had to go into the water with him. He took my bra and tied a medicine into it and left if to flow down the river. He instructed me to return to the mine and not to look back, and I never did. I left him behind, doing more stuff. Little did I know that I was digging my own grave?

He told me that our daughter was affected. This was true, because at this time she was having a vaginal discharge, which could not be cured by the doctor. So I allowed him to give her the medicine and cut her. She cried, and it hurt me very much. Thank you Lord Jesus for forgiving me. I couldn't control myself. I was possessed by demons. Daughter, I'm sorry, I did not know what I was doing. I had no control over myself. Now I can see, and follow Jesus, and Jesus alone. My one comfort is that Jesus forgives me.

This witchdoctor told me that terrible things were happening to me at night and I was tormented by these things, so I endured detestable practices in an attempt to be free, but nothing made my life better until I allowed Jesus to come into and stay in my heart. Thank you Jesus!

We travelled a long way

This witchdoctor said that dwarfs were having sexual intercourse with me during the night and were causing the vaginal discharge I had. He instructed me to find fat from dwarfs to smear on myself in the evening. He said that when the dwarf approaches to have sex, he would smell the fat, think it was another dwarf and run away. He said that this would protect me. Surely it would have thought I was a female dwarf and continue to approach me? This is likely.

He also said that witches had used an animal from the sea to cast a spell on me, so he needed the same animal to make a medicine with. He found one of these animals dead, burned and pounded it, and gave me a medicine made from it to drink. How did he know these things? Do witchdoctors have contact with witches? Probably.

Nothing made my life better until I allowed Jesus to come and stay in my heart. Thank you Jesus!

Financial abuse

I mentioned earlier that I gave a lot of money to the various witchdoctors. For example I gave about 300 pounds to one of them for some medicine. It is not possible to give the exact figures of the money I spent on those liars (as my father use to call them). As many as they were, each one charged a consultation fee and treatment fee. I knew that they were not helping me but why did I continue going to them? I had no control of myself. This happens when evil spirits possess people. They are spiritual forces that draw a person into what they want. They take total control of a person, the five senses, incuding the brain.

Readers, please understand that such people are like the deaf. Whatever you say to them may not help them to help themselves. They are totally incapable of changing themselves. Nothing changed my life for the better until I demonstrated my seriousness to follow and serve Jesus Christ alone. I was so desperate for release.

I once consulted a man who was known to be a prophet of God. I do not know whether he was a true prophet or not. He prayed and gave me a medicine to drink, the ones you buy from the chemist. I do not understand how he was able to describe my parent's bedroom in detail, as he had never seen it.

He said, "This is the bedroom of the culprit." However the lady who accoumpanied me to this man said, "oh no he means a distant relative, the one you know." The prophet gave me the Bible to open and as he was explaining he was holding a stick looking in the Bible. He told me to make a sacrifice to God by burning flour as he stood and prayed to God. He charged some money, but not very much. After all this trouble and searching, my life never changed for better until the day I said, "Yes to Jesus."

I DID NOT KNOW THAT MY MUM WAS A WITCH

My mum's evil activities.

I apologise to my husband and daughter for the problems and distress that my mum's actions have caused in our family. Should I have known that my mum was a witch, I would have kept them well away from her.

If I had known about mum's activities, I would have kept away from other people. My mum was responsible for the evil things that happened around me. She had decided to kill me, and God protected me, though I was not born again at that time. Thank you Jesus!

I became the target of the council of witches under the leadership of my mum. Read chapter 5. For example they used a certain strategy, to allow me to build, raise money and accumulate properties.. then I loose it. Once I had managed to invest about £5, 000. The trust that held my money collapsed, thank you Lord you warned me in advance. I told the agent on time not to re-invest the money, but he did. All the money was gone. Thank you Lord for recovering part of it.

I could not know my mum's intentions. I took my husband and child to my home to show them to my family. I thought that my parents would be happy to see my family. What a mistake! Could I have avoided it? I could not read their minds. After a day in their home my dad called me in and said, "We accept that you are married to this man, although you did it without our permission. We must get something. How much is he going to give us?"

I told my father that our money was combined, no dowry would be paid, but we could help them anytime when they were in need of money. He would not agree to this, and continued "These men take you, play with you and then leave you, he must pay!" I reminded my father that two men had already given them money and I was not prepared to trade with my body. He had to back down. He could not deny the truth.

Another time he asked me if "this man" was living from my money. It seems that the main issue concerning my dad was not my happiness or my well being, but one of money and financial gain. I understood that we were not welcome there. We stayed for two days and my husband suggested that we should leave. I chose to follow him and we left. Did they bless or curse us? How did my mum feel when she realised that in fact I was married legally to a European man, after she had given me away to the commander of the demons. Now I know why she never bought our daughter even a small present - not even touching or carrying her. What went on inside her…She never showed any concern about my future. All she wanted was my support. Truly, the love of money is the source of evil. Can this be the trick Satan used to get my mum to give me away to the demons?

Things start to go wrong for us

We returned to our home. We began to have more silly minor arguments. Friends became involved in our family life, and my husband began to leave us in the house and go out. His reasons being was that I did not like his friend, Mark, or that I was bullying him.

Again somebody encouraged me to go for another witchdoctor consultation by reminding me, "You are an African, not European and you should not forget this." I loved my husband very much, and I vowed to live with him till "death do us part." However I became weak and agreed to give the witchdoctors another try. This time through their divination they all knew that a spell was cast between my husband and I to divorce. Could I have avoided this?

The Lord then revealed a crucial

piece of information. This was an impossible situation to avoid; I had been covenanted to the Devil's agent, the demon Commander at the age of three.

I can not remember what happened to me at the age of three, I know that my mum had a medicine called Duiwel's druk (Devils's drops), which she put in the water for washing one of her grand children "to protect him against dirty things (evil)." This medicine is sold at the pharmacists. I refused to use them to bath my daughter with it when I was advised to.

DID THE WITCHDOCTORS HELP OR HURT ME?

I have said that I can not write about many of my encounters with them. They knew all about my misfortunes. They took my money and clothes, made me to do all horrible things in dirty places, cut my body, made me to work physically hard, deceived me into believing that my mum was not evil, they sexually abused me and added to my problems. What did the witchdoctors do to me? They hurt me! Thank you Jesus for setting me free from those demons!

Readers, you know that if by any chance you have had contact with these people, even by something as simple as reading the horoscopes, merely going in and out of church will not help you to be free. You should be honest, stop wasting your time, confess your sin, and ask Jesus to forgive you, preferably ask somebody to agree with you in this. Then you must attend the special deliverance services; they specifically address the problems you may be having. Participating in the Holy Communion is good, however, you may have waited on the LORD long enough. Now its time to get up, carry your mat and walk.

Deliverance requires engagement in Spiritual warfare. Demons need a different approach if they have to be cast out. Be prepared to wait on God. This can take some time. Only God can turn things around, and you can be happy again. He does this through His annointed servants. Seek God, and be prepared to build His Kingdom with all your heart. Rise up against the kingdom of darkness. God will wipe your tears. He did it for me. Now I'm serving happily in His Kingdom.

If the church you're attending is not helping you to come out of your problems, it is time to start to look around, ask God to send you to a church where His presence is manifested by miracles, signs and wonders. But you must be prepared to wait on God and put your faith into practice. Remember, "without faith it is impossible to please God." He sees everything; therefore He cannot be mocked. He is the only way out! Remember, when you are free you will be happy and then you can easily worship the Lord and prepare for Heaven.

CHAPTER 3

WHEN MY HUSBAND WALKED IN AND OUT OF OUR MARRIAGE

I don't regret marrying you

I remember that we had a very happy marriage for the first three years. We never upset each other, or went to bed angry, and we shared the responsibility of bringing up our daughter, Nicola. We chose to live in Africa for some time, then we later moved to Namibia, not knowing the plans of the enemy.

There was in fact a good reason for us to go to Africa, for it was here that I met our Lord Jesus Christ. God, through my mum and other agents, allowed the Devil to attack me so that I would draw closer to Him.

Because of the demons that my mum had invited to enter and live in me, I now know, and understand why problems followed wherever I went, and curses followed both my husband and me. My parents, grand parents and great- grandparents did not please God. My mum made a covenant with the Devil concerning me. She gave me to the commander of the demons as a wife, so that I should never have a human husband. Further explanation is in *chapter 4.*

However, God Almighty, who created the heavens and the earth, and who knew me before I was created in my mother's womb, refused to allow the enemy, that is, the Devil and his agents to destroy me. At some stage He showed me His love and in His mercy He gave me my husband. Certainly this was the work of God, for at that time I was not born again and I did not live for God. However, He made the impossibilities happen. None of my family knew about my marriage but my husband's family accepted me, showed love for me and cared for me. These were things I did not get from my own relatives.

I knew that my mother-in-law was not very pleased by the news that we were leaving Britain. In my mind we had to go to Africa, so that my husband could be influenced by the society there to believe in God, love Him and to live accordingly. I hoped that he would stop drinking, smoking and take a responsible role in his family. My expectations were very high, I did not realize the depth of the problems he was causing by confessing to be an Atheist. Little did I know how serious it is to deny the existence of God. We both loved each other, but we did not know that we were building a house on the sand and when the first rain came it would be washed away, unless God by

His merciful intervention rescued it. I desperately wanted my husband to change and I ended up making a mistake, by trying to change him myself and not to ask God. Only God in the name of Jesus is able to save and change people.

This is how it started. We began to have some minor arguments about my husband coming back home late. I can remember him telling me that, his friend said, "I was a slave driver." I worked very hard so that we could have enough money. I financially assisted my husband to start an electronics business, something he is good at and together we ran this business from home, to avoid the high costs incurred by paying rent for premises. We were both happy about this. The oscilloscope he used to diagnose faults was purchased out of my own investment money before we got married. I was working as a schoolteacher and also helping with collections and deliveries of TVs, videos etc. after school. Our business was flourishing, through my contacts in the city and a little advertising. We also got a licence to operate a metered taxi. We had two cars and we bought another car for me to use for work. At the end of the day three cars were parked on the driveway of our lovely home, that had a beautiful garden and a swimming pool.

My husband was working very long hours and his friends resented this, as they could not spend time with him. When we went out to dine with them, I used to insist that we should return home earlier, so that my husband could work the next day and his friends did not like this. My husband ignored their protests for a while but later he became influenced by them. They started to discuss me in drinking places. He was later influenced by them and believed it when they called me a slave driver.

Despite this, my husband loved me, he always said, "Zola I love you, I don't regret marrying you." Then he would hug both our daughter and I.

However, something strange was happening in the bedroom. I woke up many times to find myself hitting him. When he asked why, I would say I was dreaming, and I really was, but I was actually punching him. I became bored with our lovemaking and I would fake orgasm, then end up in the toilet masturbating. This was disgusting, I don't know how it started, but it goes back to when I was twelve years old, when I became sexually active. This evil spirit has made itself to be accetable as "normal" in this world. People have accepted it as a normal practice. This can not be excluded from sexual immorality, which God in His Word classifies as sin. Thank you Jesus I am free from that Spirit. Now, I use my fingers for good purposes. When demons were cast out of me I received deliverance in this area also. Eversince the Lord set me free, He allowed my body to die in flesh and alive in Spirit.

It might sound odd to write about this, however as already stated in the introduction of this book, God wants to deliver many women and men from this evil spirit, especially those who are born again and who are still gripped by this habit. One day, a sister in Christ said to me "what else can I do?" She did not realise that she was committing that which is immoral. I continued to pray and to ask God to open her eyes and He did. Yes, the Lord has allowed me to have contact with both men and women who are attacked in this way. Another sister in Christ did not know that this was not of God when she commented, "I can't help it, my husband is not well..I use a vibrator... I bought it in England."

Readers, men and women, this

habit is not of God. Therefore, I'm not ashamed to expose the works of the Devil for the Glory of Jesus Christ. God wants us to be holy, for He is holy. This may seem a "minor" sin compared to the sin of fornication, but as you know, sin is sin. There is no big sin and small sin. This sin in your life could be preventing your miracle from coming to pass. I now know that this was another form of demonic attack. I used to feel tired in the evening therefore I didn't satisfy my husband. My excuse was always that I was tired because I was working so hard. See the report Satan painted on my husband's mind on page 89.

My husband's friends did not care that he had difficulty getting up for work after a late night. Why should they anyway? We were paying the business bills from the salary I earned from my teaching job. My husband was happy with this, so who cared? I did. However, I admit I failed to deal with this problem appropriately but I learned a valuable lesson from it. Steve, who was running a sheeben, selling alcohol from his home without licence, said to my husband, concerning me, "leave her she is not worth it"... My husband told me this when he was justifying his reasons for wanting to close the business and join "the boys" as he called these men who he was drinking with.

Why did they get so involved in our family matters? Satan uses people to steal, destroy and kill human beings. He uses those who are close to easily reach his target. This was a good warning, now I am very careful about people who are close to me. Readers test the hearts of those who are close to you.

I can remember my husband saying that he was going to start a music band with one of his friends, who had his own business like my husband's, repairing electronics equipment. However he was not very good at it and he began to bring his customers' goods to my husband to repair. He then made his own profit from his customers; he eventually worked as an agent, bringing business to us. Little did we know he had something in his heart? I was upset about this band issue and would not entertain it at all. I remember saying to him; I married you because you were a TV engineer and not a guitar player in a band.

But why did I write a letter to explain my feelings while we were living together in our home? Was the situation so bad that we could not discuss issues sorrounding our home? So, the enemy first cut communication lines in families, then other attacks follow. But by then there isn't much that can be done as the discussion platform is destroyed.

When he failed to convince my

husband to close down our business and begin singing in the pubs to earn a living, he suggested that they merge the businesses. My husband agreed to this, and our business name was changed from Quintronics to Telstar. This didn't work for long, and he pulled out to sell mobile phones. Because of this man I was no longer part of the business. My husband talked about, "his business."

I opened the door for the strangers to enter our home

I introduced my husband to Steve, and then Steve introduced us to Chris. They became my husband's friends and started saying negative things about me to him. Both Steve and Chris later apologised, but the damage was already done and they did not even attempt to put things right between my husband and I. We suffered in different ways. I was tormented by the demons.

He had no money. We were separated. I had to bring up our daughter by myself. He had nothing to offer us. We both went through a very hard time.

These men encouraged my husband to leave us. Our daughter had to be separated from her dad whom she had loved for years. But, I forgave them, because God says we must forgive, vengeance is His. My husband and I could not understand each other, although we were not fighting. He ultimately moved out of our home. I was frustrated. I needed help. My biggest mistake was to go out and talk about the following story. The Devil twisted my version and it appeared that I had accused my husband of being a homosexual. I did not but I was never given the opportunity to defend myself.

This is the first time I write about what actually happened that evening. Tension between my husband and I was building up. My husband left with one of his so called friends and I said to him, "if you go out tonight this marriage is finished." I didn't mean it, I just wanted him to be with us. When he returned I was sitting in the living room. He passed me without speaking and went into the bedroom. It was about 12.30 am the phone rang and he picked it up. I listened to the conversation on the extension in another room. God has forgiven me for this. I shouldn't have listened. The caller was this man. He said, "What did Zola say?" "Nothing" replied my husband. He then said, "I'm sure she has now accepted, why don't you come back?" My husband then said "I don't know, I'll think about it." He then put the phone down. A few minutes later my husband called this man back and said, "I've changed my mind, I'm coming now."

I was very shocked by this invitation at that time, so I quickly ran to the living room before my husband passed through on his way out. I sat where he could see me. As he walked past I called out to him, "Dave!" He looked back, smiled and walked out through the back door. I heard the sound of the car driving away. I phoned this man's house. He picked up the phone and said, "Hello, hello, I'm waiting", (in a very friendly and giggly voice).

Another time before this happened; I was paying the mortgage, and working in our business, collecting and delivering Tvs, so that we could make more money. I did not want my husband to go out with Chris and I said, "if you leave me you won't find us here when you get back." They left anyway so we went to sleep in a sitting room at my friend's mum's home. When we returned the next day he was not at home. That was a Sunday afternoon. We went to sleep without him. The next afternoon I went to look for my husband. I went to this man's shop, and he was there, serving his customers. So I drove to his house and my husband was there, sleeping.

The pain was too much to endure

I realised that something was not right in my family. My husband stopped talking to me. He came back again and I remember hearing Chris saying, "you must phone Hazel and Houses, they have a house for you to rent." We tried in vain, to merge all our differences.

My husband tried to rescue our marriage. He engaged a "so called" marriage counsellor, and he paid her money. He wanted her to help us save our marriage. I never went to see that woman again after she told me that she was going to help us to part and divide the property peacefully, because the marriage wasn't working. I told her that we came to her to help us save our marriage, and that my husband is my husband "till death do us part." I repeated our wedding vows. See below:

And now David I ask that you repeat after me in this solemn promise:
I call upon these persons here present, to witness, that I, do take thee Zola, to be my lawful wedded wife
To have and to hold, from this day forward
For better for worse, for richer for poorer
In sickness and in health, to love and to cherish,
TILL DEATH DO US PART AND TO THIS I PLEDGE MYSELF

Zola, say after me:

I call upon these persons here present, to witness, that I, do take thee

David, to be my lawful wedded husband, To have and to hold, from this day forward
For better for worse, for richer for poorer
In sickness and in health, to love and to cherish
TILL DEATH DO US PART AND TO THIS I PLEDGE MYSELF IN THE NAME OF THE FATHER, SON AND HOLY SPIRIT.

Now I know that if I had known the Lord at that time, things might not have gone as far as they did. However, I got one of my relatives involved. She phoned this man and asked if he was straight. I do not know whether she wanted to know if he was gay or she used a word without thinking about its implications. Perhaps, this man told my husband about this question. That could be the reason my husband accused me of calling him a gay. This is something I never said. In frustration, I also phoned this man and threatened him. I told him that he would pay for the damage and pain he had caused, even if it was with his blood.

I was suferring as a result of his direct involvement with our family. I didn't think that could be interpreted as me wanting to kill him. I then received a call from the police, wanting an explanation for my behaviour. I sent a message, "This man must get out of our marriage affairs." He was advised to get security guards for himself if he was concerned about his safety, the police couldn't provide such protection. He did just that.

On one occasion I said to him, "You can have my husband as your wife." I did not mean he was gay. I was totally fed up of his level of control over of my husband. However, I never, then or at any time, accused my husband of being gay. I never even suspected that. The Devil made up this story and my husband used it in his claims for wanting to divorce me.

When forces of darkness are destroying a family, they take control of all those around that family. As we didn't have the protection of the blood of Jesus, there's little or nothing we both could have done. We needed the mercy of God!

My husband who did not regret marrying me, moved to that house.

My husband took one suitcase full of his clothes and moved to another house. Our daughter and I were allowed to go to see him, and he came home regularly to see us. Twice he tried to stay over, but would then jump up in the middle of the night and leave. The demon commander refused him to have any contact with me. This evil spirit confessed this later. Read the next chapter. When we went to see him, he never asked us to leave, but I would go back to our own house, because that was our home. One evening I went to the house where my husband was living, and through the window I saw two girls. I lost my temper, took out my wedding ring and threw it at him. I was with my friend and we laughed at this, it didn't click to me that our home was being destroyed.

He found business premises, through an acquaintance of mine; he began to live there. A certain woman was living in the basement of this workshop that he was renting. She was a casual worker at a butcher's. She got involved with my husband. I went to meet her and advised her to find herself a husband, because the one she was seeing was MINE.

I went to the family that offered my husband this workshop hoping to get sympathy and help. They were married.

That was another mistake I made. Anyway, they asked him not to live in the workshop. My other acquaintance that I introduced to my husband offered him a room in his house, to live with this other woman. This hurt me very much, but it taught me a very valuable lesson.

Satan knows the word of God. He knows that adultery is acceptable as a valuable reason for divorce. Therefore these evil spirits are very quick to act in this way so that there would be a justification for a divorce. For me it did not work well, because I knew already that Satan was behind my husband's down fall.

That is why he was quick to provide that woman for him. The bible says, *"The law rules over people as long as they live."* **(Romans 7:2)** This is true no one can deny this. This is the reason why those who break the laws are sent to prison or charged. The word of God continues:

"A married woman for example is bound by law to her husband as long as he lives; but if he dies, then she is free from the law that bound him to her. So then, if she lives with another man while her husband is alive, she will be called and adulteress, but if her husband dies, she is legally a free woman and does not committ adultery if she marries another man." **(Romans 7:3)**

Although there is no reference to men, I suppose this applies to them too. These verses contain the same words that my husband and I vowed …Only death would do us part. We meant it that day and I held on to our vows during those difficult times, when Satan tried to destroy our home.

One evening, I went to the house where they were living, I wanted to hit that woman. I left our daughter sleeping alone in the house. My husband's car was not there. It was very cold so I waited in my car under the trees. I waited for a long time and they did not come back so I went home to check on our daughter. While I was away they returned. I knocked at the doors and banged on the windows. I harassed them. He did not open the door for me so I punctured all four tyres on his car with a nail.

I had just paid for the repairs to his car, and now he was driving another woman around. This was extremely cruel and it hurt me deeply. My own husband, who did not regret marrying me opened the window and threw water over me, as if I was a dog. I picked up a small stone and hit him with it. He came out with a broomstick and as he was about to hit me on my head, when I shielded myself with my hand. He pushed me against the cement brick wall of the house and held my head. He was trying to bang me against this wall, and I cried. Another man called out his name and he stopped. He had pulled my braided hair and I was bleeding. He called the police to remove me. The woman was watching! Lord Jesus, deal with her and her next generations. The Devil uses other women or men to destroy existing marriages.

As you read this book, may you not be a weapon of Satan to destroy what God has joined together. If the Devil is trying to destroy your marriage using other humans, all you have to do is "resist him, and he will flee." Do not give up! Remember, your wedding vows and put the Word of God into practice; *"What God has joined together let no man put asunder."* **(Matthew 19:6)**

The police advised me to open a case of adultery against him. I did not know that it is not a criminal offence according to human law. I left it to the police anyway. I claimed maintenance through the court, but later I cancelled it because we had reconciled. The next week-end we went out for a drink. We met the policeman who came to the scene. A few weeks after that he filed for divorce.

The divorce summons

When I received divorce summons, Pastor Nigel, Pastor Katie and Sister Marge were sitting with me in our living room. There was a knock at the door and a very strange looking man was standing there, carrying some papers. I cannot remember his first words. He said he was the court messenger and he asked me to sign to verify that I had received the documents. He informed me that I had two weeks in which to defend myself. I knew that I had not done anything wrong, therefore would not be frightened by a court messenger's visit.

I looked at the summons briefly, and passed them on to one of the Pastors. We prayed and I immediately felt a sense of peace. I loved my husband very much and did not want a divorce. The next day I took the summons to church.

Pastor Sandy lifted them up to God and cancelled them spiritually in the name of Jesus. She said, "The courts operate differently to the spiritual realms so you have to engage a solicitor to reply to the summons." "Lord", I screamed, "where will I get the money from to pay a solicitor?" The Lord provided a born again sister, who is an advocate. She agreed to handle the case spiritually. This was a miracle. I did all the typing of the documents that had to be sent out. It was very hard to do this but I knew that the blood of Jesus protected every piece of paper handled by her.

My solicitor wrote back to his

solicitors and requested proof of those accusations. Satan told my husband lies and made him feel that I did not want him. As an act of faith I destroyed all his solicitors' letters. I kept my response records in our computer. Listed below are his reasons for wanting to divorce me, which also made him to walk away from our home for seven years:

" I argued with him consistently
" I insulted him infront of his friends
" I refused to allow him to make decisions regard ing his own business
" I interfered with the running of his business
" I threaten to leave him
" I left our home
" I refused to let him have friends
" I accused him of being homosexual

" I assaulted him

" I hired people to assault his friends
" I failed to show love and affection
" He therefore requested the court to condone his adulterous actions

My husband seemed to have gone through hard times as well. When I read the reasons he gave for wanting divorce, it became clear that he was unhappy. Satan had bombarded him with all these thoughts and feelings in order to try to divide and destroy us. He used the divide and rule strategy. To those who are attacked in the same way, you need to know the truth. Readers be wise!

I decided to attend the court hearing with my solicitor because I wanted to pray against the spirit of divorce in the courtroom. When I met the lady, who was representing my husband. I thought, "How dare you?

You are a woman. What do you think you're doing? Have you seriously given thought to the fact that you're contributing to destroying a family that God has set up? Get ready to fight with God!" After binding the spirits of divorce and casting it out in the name of Jesus, I claimed victory over our marriage in the name of Jesus. I stood on **Matthew 19: 6**, *"What God has joined together, let no man put asunder."* Not even my husband or myself has that right.

I was a new convert that time. I didn't know the Word of God very much. So I held on the Word I knew. I managed to get near to my husband's representative and I asked her if she was aware of what she was doing? I assured her that she was going against God's plan. I reminded her that she was not present when the Lord joined me to my husband and only death would us part, in the Name of Jesus. Is this not true? Do brides and grooms invite solicitors to their weddings? I wish they could. Why do they get them involved later? Who are the wedding witnesses? Ministers? Why are people so quick to forget about them when problems arise in homes arise? Are they too far away? If so, why?

At that time everybody went into court. I was sitting at the back praying, mostly in the Spirit, I felt the presence of God in me; I was fasting and praying that week. I reminded the Lord that He is the Judge and I wanted to see justice done immediately. Our names were not yet called when the court had to be dismissed for lunch. Praise the Lord! After lunch I was sitting in the waiting room, and there was no sign of my solicitor, or my husband's solicitor. I sat there thanking God for that victory.

We all went in and when it came to our turn, both solicitors were still absent. Another solicitor from my husband's representative's firm asked that the case be adjourned with costs. I left the courtroom full of joy, praising the Lord. A short time later, my husband and I went out for dinner. He indicated that there was no need for us to divorce and therefore we didn't have to go to court the following Monday.

That Monday, I went to see him where he was living with that woman, because I needed assurance that the divorce was cancelled. He asked me to telephone his solicitors. I said, "Hello, this is Mrs Quinnen, my husband would like to speak to you." I passed over the receiver and he said, "I have been telling my wife that I have cancelled the divorce and she doesn't believe me that's the reason I'm phoning." She said, "okay", and dropped the phone.

Think for a minute…How did I feel when I looked at my husband and the woman he was sleeping with? It hurt, however, I knew that he was innoscent. Evil spirits were at work.

Later God healed that internal hurt. Soon after that we agreed to return to England, there was hope for our marriage, I Idid not know that some demons, were still in my stomach. (*See Chapter 6*)

Readers, should there be an intruder in your family that God has given you, a man or a woman, do not be hurt or panic. Go back to your wedding vows. Read and make sense of them. None of the couple has a right to call divorce, as long as you both shall live. I held on the truth that my husband and I declared before God and many witnesses; *"To have and to hold, from this day forward, For better for worse, for richer for poorer, In sickness and in health, to love and to cherish Till death do us part and to this I pledge myself in the name of the Father, Son and Holy spirit, Amen."*

Why do people rush to solicitors when the bad times come? It may seem stupid to ask this question. The answer is simple, the pain gets too much. The evil spirit whispers a message, "you better come out of it, you'll find someone better." That's a lie! The fact that in marriage couples vow, "for better for worse, for richer for poorer, in sickness and in health." It is already predicted that these times will come, sooner or later. However, they are not from God. How does God feel when believers go to for divorce after He had said in His word, "I hate divorce" Is this not a violation of His Word? Why should the forces of darkness be allowed to win? Surely when they see this happen, they laugh and celebrate. When I committed myself to do the work of God, He took away the pain, anger, and evil spirits, that were destroying our family. Perhaps there's a need to look at the marriage vows and the law. Believers, we have a job to do!

When God sees the desperate and

humble hearts, He takes away the internal pain. Although some things may be in the process of being solved, it doesn't mean He will not sought them out. He deals with the major issues first…demons…the internal pain. But one has to accept and acknowledge that the situation is beyond their control. Then give it to Jesus to solve it and refuse to interfere by taking your attention away from it. This is possible when you replace that attention with work in the Kingdom of God. This requires a lot of sacrifies and commitment.

Remember when you modify behaviour, you can't remove one without substituting it with the other. Should you do so the vaccuum remains needing to be filled up. If the new filling is not done, the possibility is bringing back the old habit. This works the same in the spititual realm. When the work of Satan is abandoned, the works of the Kingdom of God should replace it and this has to be at a higher level. This is what I just did to overcome! The problem with us can be … we don't want to do much for God, but He must sought us out while we are in our homes, sometimes still doing the same things we were doing while we were in the world. It does not work like that. There has to be a remarkable change. There's a lot to give up….

PART TWO

CHAPTER 4

I GAVE MY HEART TO JESUS AND HE REVEALED THE TRUTH

The beginning of the healing process

I decided to leave Namibia. I applied for work in South Africa hoping that, as I hold Master's degree in Special Education and I am South African by birth I would get it easily. My application was acknowledged and I was told that I would be informed later. That gave me hope I waited for the appointment, but heard nothing.

I had never been to the Province I wanted to live in, so during summer holiday I decided to visit this place. I left our daughter with my sister in Christ. As I was leaving her she advised me that on my return, we should go to a crusade, that is, church services organised by Born Again Christians. She said that it was here that my problems could be solved. I didn't answer her, because I had had too much torture from my husband and I just wanted to get away. She was right!

I travelled by coach and arrived at Potchefstroom the next day, I was dreadfully sad in my heart. I managed to book myself in a hotel, despite the fact that the area was predominantly European. The next morning I went to some offices to make enquiries. All the workers I met there were European but that didn't discourage me, as I thought they were ready to integrate with other races.

When I left the offices, I was convinced that it was too early to expect to be appointed there. The atmosphere was still the "old South Africa" I knew. I went to buy a newspaper to occupy myself that evening. I saw a book called "Men, Women and Relationships, Making Peace with the Opposite Sex." (Gray 1993). I bought the book hoping to find information, which would help me to understand how I failed to keep my husband at home.

The next morning I was on my way back to Namibia. After boarding the coach, I continued to read this book. Internally I was very hurt. I have no words to describe how hurt I was. I felt as if I had wounds inside. And every time I took a breath, the sharp pain made me to think; it was better to die. A man who was sitting next to me started a conversation by asking about the book I was reading.

We continued to chat and he invited me to the same Crusade my friend had spoken of. He gave me a programme and some leaflets. I didn't take it seriously; I was fed up of these people who said that God would restore my family. The pain inside was unbearable. This was an overnight journey, so we arrived the next morning.

When I went to collect our daughter, I showed this sister the programme and she said it was the same meeting she had invited me to. On the 30th September 1996 I went to this Crusade. A woman preacher was preaching from

Matthew 11: 28-30.

"Come to me, all ye that labour and Are heavy laden, and I will give you Rest. Take my yoke upon you, and Learn of me: for I am meek and lowly In heart: and ye shall find rest unto Your souls. For my yoke is easy, and My burden is light." She shouted

verse 28 and said

"The Lord Jesus Christ is talking to You tonight. If you want to give Your hearts to Him come to the front Now, He is here."

I ran to the front immediately. Other people started filling in the space at the front. We prayed the sinner's prayer led by another woman. While we were standing there the preacher asked if we wanted to be baptised by the Holy Spirit and we were invited to remain. She prayed and she was quiet and then said, "receive the Holy Spirit, open your mouths and speak." Another lady touched my lower jaw and I started speaking in tongues. It was very strange, I couldn't control my speech and I didn't understand what I was saying. Every body there received the Holy Spirit. Now I understand that the preacher was in the Spirit because I have been in the Spirit myself.

At this meeting people were invited to talk to the pastors, especially those who had special needs. I went, but instead of talking I was crying and I told this Pastor that my life was destroyed, that I had no reason to live. My money was finished. I was selling my furniture in order to raise money to survive. I told him that I had been losing money, giving it to the witchdoctors who were saying that they could remove the bad luck and I could get back everything I had lost, including my husband. The Pastor asked me if I had any stuff from the witchdoctors in my house, because now that I was in Christ I was a new creation all the old things had passed. God had forgiven me from worshipping idols (witchdoctors). All those things had to be removed from my home and my life.

I arranged to pick up the Pastor at lunchtime. I showed him all the medicine planted in the house and the yard. He dug everything out. He prayed, anointed the house with olive oil and took these herbs away. These were burnt at the Crusade. I felt very happy inside. I had hope for life again. I sold my guitar that I had brought to sing and worship the Lord, so now I had some money.

After the Crusade, I began to attend one of the churches in the area. There was no actual church building so Jonny offered his house. An extension was made with zinc and plastics and people were meeting there everyday. The Pastor, and his wife visited our daughter and I sometimes. They prayed with us. I gained understanding about the Lord Jesus Christ.

My love for him grew. I just followed the teaching in the Bible as it is and I did everything that I was shown in the Bible. I started to pay my tithes, although this was very hard because I had two mortgages to pay which took almost all my salary so I was left with nothing to give towards the work of the Lord. The teaching about giving continued anyway. It hurt me that I couldn't give 10% of my salary before deductions. I thank the Lord now, because I don't have loans to pay back and I am able to give my money towards the work of the Kingdom of Jesus Christ and I have never failed to get what I need.

My life started changing. I spent most of my time in this church. I learned to call out and cry to the Lord and pray. I stopped phoning my friends who deceived me. I made new friends from the church. Whenever we met we talked about the Word of God. A miracle happened to me one day. There was a teaching about baptism by full immersion after repentance. I gave my name and on the 19th October 1996 I was baptised as according to the book of;

Matthew 28: 19;

"Go then to all peoples everywhere And make them my disciples: baptise

Them in the name of the Father, The Son and the Holy Spirit."

I was then given a certificate. I was happy afterwards and I served the Lord with all my heart. I never kept quiet about my salvation. I told everybody, and one of my friends also accepted the Lord and was baptised in the Holy Spirit with the evidence of speaking in tongues.

I can remember one Sunday in the service, I wanted to give a testimony about what the Lord had done for me. I was testifying that my husband took me to the house where he was living in adultery with that woman. He kept talking to our duaghter and I all the time in her presence. He was very affectionate and this woman left the sitting room to sit in another room. I was giving this testimony when suddenly I couldn't control my speech, now I understand that I was in the Spirit.

I saw a vision of people suffering from AIDS. As I continued speaking I said, "God is very angry about the sin of sexual immorality. A way of stopping this sin from continuing is by launching, World Unity Body of the Married Persons, an association under the umbrella of Jesus Christ. Newly married people can register with this body, which will be continuously interceding for these homes. When the Devil comes with his attacks on any home, all the members will wage spiritual warfare to support either the man or the woman to ensure that the Lord protects that family."

After I had said all this, I fell down

with my face to the floor and my whole body was shivering (jerking movement from head to toe). Now I understand that I was in the Spirit and the demons were manifesting, but nobody took any notice. The pastor carried on praying. This continued for some time. It was very noisy, some people were groaning, others were crying, and then it was quiet. I stood up feeling tired.

I visited another church

The next Sunday, when the morning service had ended, I did not want to go home, I just wanted to be in the presence of the Lord. With a sister in Christ in my car, I drove straight to this church for another morning service. To my relief it was still on when we arrived. That afternoon there was to be a women's fellowship meeting at 3pm. I was very happy because this was another service to attend. I just wanted to hear the word of God preached. It comforted me, it gave me hope, I felt better, and I understood all God's promises to human kind.

I picked up my friend from her house and we drove to the women's fellowship meeting. During the service Pastor Sandy introduced another Pastor called Katie, and invited her to share about missions. This lady stood up. She looked very young, but as she spoke there was something in her voice. She sounded very bold, and caught my attention.

When she had finished she returned to her seat, which was in front of me. Another sister in Christ was praying, it might have been one of the Pastors. Suddenly I burst into tears. I cried loudly to the top of my voice like a baby. I don't know whether other people were crying or not but I just couldn't stop. It was not me crying, it was the demons. I have heard similar cries from other people in church.

When the meeting finished and Pastor Sandy was walking down the aisle. Pastor Katie stopped her and said, "I think this sister needs a prayer." They both laid their hands on me and prayed. I stopped crying. It was very painful. I had no particular reason to cry. I had been very hurt several times by my husband's refusal to return home. I knew deep down in my heart that he would return to us. I trusted God.

I walked out of the church and a sister, who also knew Pastor Katie, introduced her to me. God always assigns someone to help solve our problems. He is faithful. He connects birds of the same feathers. I invited Pastor Katie to stay at our house. We arranged for me to pick her up the following Monday afternoon. We then left the church.

The following day, as it was

agreed, I drove to collect Pastor Katie. After a while she walked into the house with Pastor Sandy. As Pastor Sandy was about to leave she gave her a scripture from the book of Isaiah and said "lead her into deliverance" and then she said to me, "go on fasting for three days." I never questioned anything. I stopped eating immediately. I did as the woman of God told me and God confirmed His word.

The first manifestations of demons in Namibia.

Day One

We all went to our bedroom and we read the scripture, there was another knock at the door. It was one of my relatives. I didn't go to meet her. Pastor Katie started to minister to her and she left. When she came back to our bedroom, we were praying. She stopped us and asked me if I had made a blood sacrifice in the house. I did not understand what she meant by this, so she explained that it meant the slaughtering of something to honour the ancestors. I told her that I had, and she had me take her to the spot where I did it. As she prayed and poured olive oil, I jumped up and screamed. They held me by my hand and we went back to my bedroom.

I was sitting on my bed as she was praying calling the name of Jesus. I jumped up and screamed. All my actions that happened were involuntarily, I couldn't hold or control my body, and as I spoke things I knew nothing about. I heard everything and I was aware of what was happening. Then, I shouted "ho- ha-ha-ha-ha, who are you? Get out of this house?" I spoke very firmly, "who are you?" I was quiet. She shouted, "in the name of Jesus, speak, who are you?" I clenched my lips and opened my eyes widely. I fell on the floor with my back and my lower body was moving up and down. The actions were different; I would stick my tongue out and swerve like a snake. I made a lot of gestures and facial expressions.

Many people from the church arrived and they were asking, "who are you?" and I wouldn't answer, and as they shouted, "talk in the name of Jesus." I answered things that I didn't know about. I had no control of my mouth or any other action but I heard and I am aware of everything that happened that day.

The information that came out was "I am the Commander. We are many." Someone asked, "How many are you?" The answer was, "We are thousands and thousands and thousands. We are not going out, Ha! Ha! (Crying, calling my mum), we are burning, they said calling another relative!" Tears were running down my cheeks.

There were many people of God present, some were praying behind me and others were taking turns commanding the demons to come out in the Name of Jesus. The demons were very stubborn and aggressive, saying, "we are not going out, she is ours we were given her." Some body asked, when did you go into her? The answer was, "when she was three years old." The people prayed and left about 3am. We all had to go to work the next day.

Day Two

I went to school as usual but I was very shocked about the previous day's events. It was my second day of fasting I drank water only. After school I went straight home. Pastor Katie told me to write down everything I could remember. I did this and I soon discovered that the sin started when I was a little girl.

I wrote everything I could remember, starting from stealing, fornicating, and worshipping idols (witchdoctors). Pastor Katie was praying, crying, and asking God to forgive me. I was sitting on our bed.

I saw a shadow and my own mum was standing in front of me.

With shock I said, "hah mum," As I was looking, I saw dust and my car overturning and I said, "my car!" My mum was standing holding a bottle with black stuff in it and I shouted, "that bottle." I saw Rachel; she appeared sitting down, facing me. I shouted, "Rachel" and cried, "mum did you kill her?" She answered me, and I asked her, "why?" She said, "money." I saw my late dad with the lump on his neck; he had the growth that was diagnosed as cancer, by the doctors. Then I saw another relative. I said, "but mum she is suffering so much." Another shadow appeared from my left shoulder, as I looked I saw Jill. She was smiling showing her teeth. Pastor Katie was standing a bit away from me. She asked for the phone and I heard her talking to Pastor Sandy. She had written everything down I had said. We went to bed.

"Zola, so many lizards on the wall."

It was after midnight, when there was a knock at the gate. It was one of my relatives. As I opened the gate, I asked what was the matter at that time of night, she didn't answer me, and she just walked into the house. Amazed, I looked at her little girl of 5 years old. She said, "Zola, so many lizards on the wall" I asked her son who said, "there are 9 lizards on the wall." As they entered the living room I asked this lady if this was true and she said, it was, and just insisted she wanted to go to sleep.

She didn't look surprised when I asked her what was she going to do. She said she was going to call the Prophet, from the church to go to the house the next day. I advised her to accept the Lord and I assured her that we would go and drive them out. She refused and insisted on sleeping. I told Pastor Katie who said, "just let her sleep, you will be alright." The next day I went to work.

Day three

Just before I left school, I received a phone message from the secretary saying that I should go straight to church and not go home. I drove to church. Pastor Sandy, Katie and Daisy were there. As Pastor Sandy looked at me I screamed at her, "who are you?" I hate you! She didn't answer she just looked at me. I said, "look, let me show you." I began jumping very high, like another group of fortune-tellers, and these are the people who believe that they have powers from their ancestors. I had consulted these people. The woman who told me about the stillbirth I had in 1978 belonged to this council. Pastor Sandy held me by my hand saying, "come and meet Jesus" and we entered the church through the back door. As I walked in I saw Jesus Christ, just as the scripture says in **Matthew 11:27** that *"No one knows the Father except the Son and those to whom the Son chooses to reveal him."* Jesus is really alive, and has been since *"He first appeared first to Mary Magdalene, from whom He had driven out seven demons."* **(Mark 16:9)**

I saw our Lord Jesus Christ This is what I saw:

He looked like He does in the pictures that show Him with a lighter brown face. He can be described as tall; I had to look up in order to see His face. He was dressed in loose cream robes. Immediately I fell on my face to the ground crying "Jesus" I pressed my face down, I couldn't look at him. Somebody turned my face to look in the direction of where Jesus was standing. I was refusing just crying, really crying. They managed to turn my head and I saw Him moving just to look at me and He did not say or do any thing. I couldn't look at Him; I couldn't bear the light that was about His face. Jesus is really alive. In whatever trouble you may be going through, He is looking at you and has all the solutions.

I was screaming, calling my mum and one of my relatives. (In fact the demons were crying as they burned from the fire of God). One of the people asked, "Who are you?" The demon answered, "I am Commander, but we are many." Somebody came next to me shouting "Commander, come out of her in the name of Jesus." I continued screaming calling my mum and this other relative. My chest was burning I asked for water. I was given water to drink.

After a long time, people were shouting, "come out in the name of Jesus, the voice asked," "where shall we go?" Somebody answered, "go to the graves where you belong." The voice out of my mouth cried, "we are many." Then it said, "you there go to Molly's grave and you go to Tom's grave, who died in a car accident nearly the same time with Rachel, and you, go to Bev's house. It's small but fill every space, and under the beds." I saw figures like crowds of people moving swiftly to different directions immediately. The kingdom of darkness is well organised like any army with different ranking officers. They have organised communication structures. They take orders from their commanders. They do exactly as they are told. They use different strategies to attack human beings. You would understand what I mean if you have heard of a 'gorilla war' and divide and rule war strategies'.

That information was true, this relative lived in a house that was small. So evil spirits know where people live. Christians, be wise demons are at work. I will not reveal more of their activities, because they are still the enemy. But I will continue to advise the soldiers of Jesus Christ of their weakest points. They should not know what we know about them. They will be wise.

However, they are weak. They call each other, "boys". That shows good team evil spirit when they are attacking their enemy, those who do the will of God - serious Christians who refuse to committ sin. The power that Jesus gave us is more than enough to destroy them.

Every time Pastor Katie stood in front of me and looked in my eyes, her eyes looked deep red like blood, and when she spoke there was an immediate response. At last the voice said, "open" and I opened my mouth. Somebody brought a rubbish bin.

I vomited clots of blood

I vomited blood with clots and it was smelly. My chest was burning inside. I moved to the prayerroom, which had a sink. I remember vomiting into the sink, a lot of blood in clots. Where did that blood come from? Why and how did it form clots? The miracle service, which was held every Thursday, was about to start. So I went to sit at the back of the church. Pastor Sandy made an altar call. One of my relatives who was called by the demons, went up for prayer and as she laid her hands on her she fell down. I went back home that evening knowing that I was possessed by evil spirits. I knew that my family was used by Satan, through his agents, demons to destroy me.

Day 4, in our house

It was the same week when I was told that this same relative had been admitted to the hospital. She sent for me to collect her belongings. I did not want to see her, so I asked another lady to take her keys to her. I waited for her in the lifts. This is where I met another Pastor, and as we talked I gave him my address. God will always make good connections when we depend on Him for everything.

A week or two later he came to our house to visit me. As he was about to leave, we prayed. The demons began to fight. I pushed him away, asking "who are you? What do you want? Go away." He held me and said, "I am a child of the Living God." I hit him, as he tried to restrain me, then I got hold of him, shook him and threw him to the ground. Where did I get such strength from? Definately I was not myself. I reached out for the phone and dialled another lady's number. As he came close to me, I screamed. Within a short period of time, this lady and her husband arrived. Pastors and other brothers and sisters in Christ also arrived to help.

The Spirit of God was moving around me. They were commanding the demons to go out in the name of Jesus. The prayers were very hot. I was screaming saying *"I'm not going out,*

Zola is my wife, her mother gave her to me." Readers, did you know that people could have spiritual husbands and wives?

I was hitting them and they had to restrain me. I was very hurt. I cried as others were twisting my fingers. I was crying, tears were running down my cheeks. I said, "I'm Zola you're hurting me." But they were trying to help me. The voice said "you're hurting this child, we are inside her stomach." Pastor Katie was crying and she came around stretched out her hand and said, "fire of the Holy Ghost, consume them." She did not touch me. I burned inside and I was screaming.

Pastor Sandy closed my ears with her fingers, oh that was the worst torture. I cried because my ears were burning with fire. The demons ignored some of the brothers and sisters who commanded them to go. They would just say, "nc" Now I know that people need the power of God to successfully do this good work.

I thank God that all this happened in Namibia. Neighbours did not complain about noise. The church members could come to our home and drive out the evil spirits without the fear of neighbours calling the police to complain about noise. Jesus and His followers drove out the evil spirits from those who were possessed. May people love one another! When neighbours are going through problems like these, which are similar to any sickness, may those who are free be helpful to them. I needed this help that time.

Zola or her mother should die in order for us to come out

The voice continued "her mother told us never to leave her until she dies. She has to die with us. We cannot go, either her mother or her should die in order for us to go out." Somebody said angrily "kill her mum." I will never forget the burning sensation I felt when Pastor Sandy closed my ears with her fingers. I cried, I chose to die and I fell on the floor. But why did I have to go through this?

Some people bent my fingers, they hurt me. I know they were trying to help but only the two pastors had the power to remove the evil spirits. When these Pastors spoke the demons answered, and they moved from one side of my tummy to another, like a baby moving in a tummy of a pregnant woman. Deliverance ministers don't have to hurt those who are in trouble seeking to be delivered. When you bind the strong men first, then you have the total control of the whole situation.

The voice continued, it insisted, *"she is my wife, I kicked David out of this house, I will not hurt her, just let me stay."* It said all the others were gone it was remaining alone. I began to physically hit those around me. I was very strong to scatter so many people. I remember holding Daisy's husband with one hand, shaking him and throwing him on the floor. I rushed to the kitchen to get a knife. I wanted to stab myself to death. They managed to stop me. People were getting very tired, the voice said, *"Pray hard I want to go out, but I'm stuck, because I came in red meat."* I saw the piece of meat; it looked like mutton, beef or goat. It was about midnight when this demon announced, "I am going out." I went to the bathroom and I vomited on the floor. The whole floor space was covered in smelly blood clots. I remember Satie washing me in the bath afterwards. Thank you Satie, you taught me to love my neighbours. I have done the same to others during deliverance. I was dreadfully tired. I remember Kim giving me porridge. I tried to eat it but

I couldn't, as my chest was very sore. The next day I tried to drink water, I could swallow but it hurt as the water went down.

Another day, the manifestations of demons in our bedroom

On another occasion I was screaming calling my mum, and two other relatives. On that day when they left they were all tired and they made me confess, "Jesus is Lord," they then led me in prayer. We took the stand of faith as we declared and believed that I was free. However, I knew that they were not gone as they said f*** words to some people who were talking.

At the deliverance service in Church

One particular day I decided to attend a special deliverance service at 10am. As I was driving to church, about to pass a T-junction, a car came from a side road at a high speed and did not stop at the stop sign. I was just a little way from the crossing. The young European lady who was driving drove in the same direction without stopping. This was an extremely near miss.

I continued on to church. I had shoes on, which I had just bought, as I went to the altar for prayer I started jerking. This jerking continued until I was free and I thought it was a manifestation of the Holy Spirit. A Pastor who was visiting the church engaged in a conversation with the demons. He asked, "what activities have you undertaken to destroy this church?" The answer was "I don't do anything, I just make Zola tired." Again the voice spoke in a third person, to show that it wasn't me speaking.

The next question was, "do you sometimes find yourself flying?" There was no answer. When he said, "manifest yourself in these shoes." I began to demonstrate the movement of a snake. I don't know how was this possible. I left the church without my shoes on, I didn't want them, so I threw them in the bin outside. Evil spirits are real, I have proved this in a very hard way indeed. Anyway, from that day I believed that I was free. I continued attending the services. I always had the jerking movements whenever I was in the Spirit, but I thought it was the manifestation of the Holy Spirit. My hands would really shiver. Yes, the demons were burning from the fire of the Holy Ghost. They could not relax as they usually did when I was in the churches with less or no fire.

The family had to know

I received a letter from my mum, and the contents were funny. I took this letter to Pastor Sandy, I read and interpreted it because it was written in my language which she did not understand. She said, "write a letter to your mum and tell her to repent." I wrote a letter, but never posted it. I was telling her that I knew what she did to me, a bit confrontational but advising her to choose Jesus.

I received a second letter from her, which was also funny. The content included the following:

Dear Baby,

(she never called me this). I am writing about what's going on. Nobody told me anything, but I can see the action. Be ashamed...

I took this letter to my Pastor,

Sandy and she told me to write to my mum and tell her about Jesus.

My second letter to Mum

This time I posted a short letter, which said

Dear mum,

I want you to know that I have forgiven you. I was always going to give you money...Repent.....

I phoned one of my relatives and told her about the visions that I had seen. Her reaction was, "Is she a witch?" I said, "I am not interpreting any thing, I'm telling you the power of Jesus." She spoke to me again another time, she was still shocked and I led her to accept the Lord.

On Thursday, the 19th of June

1997, I returned from Church in the evening and there was an urgent message, telling me not to go to sleep without phoning my relatives. I immediately phoned the same relative, she answered and asked, "have you heard what has happened at your home?" I replied, "no." She then said to me, "your parents are dead!" I asked her what had happened? She told me that it was not clear and she would call again. I remembered the words that demon had spoken, "One of them should die" and I believed that I was truly set free, because my mum was dead.

Some people may argue against listening to the information given by evil spirits. Yes, it can be unreliable and misleading most of the times. Satan is the father of lies, no one can believe what they say. However, when they are under pressure, burning from the fire of the Holy Spirit, they unintetionally release some information. God allows them to do this. Evil spirits are real be wise!

I still wondered why did my dad also die? I never thought I would loose my parents in a day. The life of an orphan! That is another topic on its own. At the end everybody I knew and trusted let me down. I trusted no one around me. I chose to live alone again- of course our daughter was always by me. I waited for God to return my husband.

Deep down in my heart I was not alone... Jesus Christ of Nazareth was always with me. I turned to Him; I spoke to Him, hoping to hear His voice saying, "cry no more, all your prayers are answered." I cried calling Him. I wanted quick answers. Sometimes things didn't happen at the times I was praying. However, He answered all my prayers. Yes, sometimes I had to wait. There is a waiting time, but who ever trusts in the Lord and live to obey His commands, will never be disappointed. I never saw my parents again. Only God knows what would have happened, had I seen them after all that painful experience? The Bible says, "He is our protector." I went to their funeral not knowing what to expect.

CHAPTER FIVE

JILL REVEALED SOME OF THEIR WITCHCRAFT ACTIVITIES

During the early evening we arrived at my parents farm for their funeral. Some brothers and sisters in Christ from the church accompanied me. My home, where I was brought up looked different. My mum was not there; she used to meet us at the door when we arrived, usually followed by my dad the man I loved. We entered the living room; the room divider, which used to display ornaments, had gone. There were chairs along each side of the living room. We were given a bedroom in which to put our luggage. There were some relatives who were moving around the house. The tune of the song, *"Be still and know that I'm*

God" remained in my mind. I felt heavy inside, but I did not cry. A family member explained what had happened to us.

Who killed my Mum and Dad that morning and why?

This is what she said;

Some boys had come to the house one evening; they were provoking my parents. The next morning they were on their way to the police to report the details of these events, when they met their death in front of their home.

One of my relatives was waiting for them in the town as they had arranged to meet at 9am and then go together to the police. When they didn't shown up by 11am, he took a taxi home. As he was walking down the hill towards the house he saw their bodies lying apart.

Their dogs ate their bodies

Their dogs were eating their bodies. He picked up my mum's bag, which had money and other documents in it and ran back to the road. He fell over and badly hurt his knee. He managed to get a lift to town and when he got out of the car he saw Jill. He told her what he had discovered; apparently he was very shocked and shaken and was crying. They went to call the police. The police and cameramen went to the farm. When they arrived at the scene the dogs were still eating the bodies. The big stones that had been used to kill them were put under their necks, and their heads were crushed and shapeless. A black cat was lying dead in front of the main building. Both dogs also died before the funeral.

We were extremely tired, so we prayed and tried to go to sleep, but I couldn't sleep well. It was very creepy.

Every time I tried to sleep I felt something touching and feeling me and I would shout, "Jesus."

The next morning we went to the spot where they died. There was just grass there. We prayed and anointed the whole area. That evening we were allowed to conduct the Vigil prayers. I can remember Jill talking to me, saying everybody thought I was going to cry. They were worried because they wouldn't know how to calm me down. I answered her bravely; I told her that there was no need to cry, because the Lord Jesus has set me free. She joined us in the prayers. We started by worshipping the Lord. We then prayed in the Spirit and in understanding, but mostly in the Spirit. When the Holy Spirit took control the noise was louder. Then it was quiet; Jill was down on her knees. She was crying. She said:

"The Lord has sent you here to come and set me free. I was in bondage

for over fifteen years. My mum told me to join her. I didn't want to but I had to join. Oh
every body feared her. She was a queen."
(She demonstrated a walk with shoulders and lifted up both hands forming brackets)

I went to sit down on the sofa and the others were still praying. She came to me and said "Tell me, how did this happen?" I shouted, "Jesus has set me free. There's power in the name of Jesus." She then asked me, "Did God show you the bad things we were doing?" I answered "yes." She continued, "Did He show you the good things?" I answered, "No." She cried and walked away from me but stayed in the same room. She then said, "you must know that those people who will be at the funeral don't like you. They say your husband treats you like a queen." I was surprised by this comment. How did they know the relationship between my husband and I.? I answered bravely, "I don't care, they are wasting their time, anyway my husband is coming." It became clear that when my husband's friends were discussing me in the pubs, the council of witches under my mum's leadership was in discussion and plotting the strategies to separate us.

To those witches who plotted my downfall, I have news for you, "Repent or perish." My Father in Heaven will deal with you, and you will reap what you sowed.

Jill just wanted to talk about these activities. Thank You Lord that one of the sisters in Christ was able to listen to her and tell me later, because I was very busy with the funeral arrangements.

One of the things I had to do was to break down the stick house I had built at the instructions of the witchdoctor. This is the same one, who told me about the stillbirth I had. How did she know about this? Now that I was a new creation in Christ, Pastor Sandy had instructed me to break down the house. I sent my sister's children to start breaking the house down. When I returned they told me that another relative had stopped them. I told one of my aunts who was also surprised about a strangled frog that she found hanging on the water tank. The relative came in at that time and he said that the house could be used as a storeroom, it didn't have to be broken down.

It was at this stage that I experienced the same feeling I had when the demons manifested, and I shouted, "It is my house, I built it with my money. I'm breaking it down, this is my life." Jill came in at that time and said to him, "leave her to do what she wants, you can hear her, she says it's her life." Thank You Lord for using her to support me. I went shopping and when I returned I found that my brothers and sisters in Christ had broken it down and burnt it to ashes. I was very happy.

Jill asked me, "How did you know that the things were kept in that house?" In fact there was just an old chest of drawers there. The whole house was empty. What ever was there was invisible. My answer was, "There's power in the name of Jesus, the Lord has showed me many things." She cried and walked away.

Jill talked to my sisters in Christ about many things. When I returned they said we had to hold a service of restoration, because Jill wanted to apologise. We held this service. The first person she went to say sorry to was the young man, who could not write his exams at the university because he was not well according to the doctor's diagnosis. He was seeing Jill in visions and crying. Thank you Jesus, this boy was born again and he accepted the apology. Jill told me she felt safe now that mum was gone. She said that she would collect her children, who were in hiding. I was thankful to the Lord, who had set her free. I never allowed myself to have long discussions with her. I don't know the reason for this, as I was not even upset by her stories. She invited us to go and pray in her house before we returned to Namibia, and we did this.

When my mum and dad died

I felt like a stranger in my own home. I had no relations with any of my relatives. I don't remember talking with them any longer. Anyway Rachel who was so close to me had died. I was alert. I made a good contribution towards the funeral costs. We prepared for the funeral. Only the next of kin were allowed to go to the funeral undertakers to view the bodies. They were not in a good condition. When the soul lives these bodies, really they become nothing.

I was fasting and praying that week. I knew the enemy was near. I couldn't trust anyone to give me food. Yes, all the people I trusted and loved disappointed me. My mum engineered my downfall! I left my home, where I grew up after the funeral, not knowing when I would see that farm again. I wanted to forget about my sad home memories. All the good things were now covered by sadness, disappointment and feelings of betrayal.

The news about my parents' death didn't shock me. This is because at that time, I didn't know what meant to have a family around. Once I was once part of a big family but I now had Jesus and our daughter as family. Even the man who had vowed infront of many witnesses never to leave me till death do us part had abandoned me. All those I trusted let me down. Perhaps it was my fault to trust people.

My friend, Jesus was far from me then, because I had not invited Him to come into my life. I do not know how I would have coped if I did not have Jesus in me, when I had to return home to bury my parents and face my relatives who sat in the council of witches, under the leadership of my mum to destroy me.

This was another challenge. I had to go and bury them. They gave birth to me. I cried often when I thought about them. The song, *"Be still and know that I am God, in thee oh Lord I put my trust."* always touched my spirit when I sang it. There was no turning back. I prepared the regiment, the soldiers of the cross. The spiritual war between the forces of darkness and the forces of light was not over…I didn't know what was waiting ahead. The Lord actually confirmed through the confession of Jill that witchcraft is real, be wise. However, the power that is in Jesus, is sufficient to destroy all the works of Satan. Together with those who came to comfort our family, we held services during day and vigils at night.

Some of the preachers read from **1 Kings 23:13-19,** the story about Naboth's vineyard. This is the man who was stoned to death because King Ahab wanted his vineyard. Dogs licked his blood but God intervened on his behalf because he was in right standing with Him. God said concerning Jezebel who was Ahab's wife, that dogs would eat her flesh. Ahab was influenced by his wife to do evil in the eyes of the Lord **(1 Kings 21:23-24).**

Why did the preachers compare my parents' death to that of Naboth? Is it because Naboth was a good, Godly man or because dogs licked his blood after he was stoned to death just like my parents or both. Were they implying that my parents were good? I shall not question the reason why God sent messengers to say that dogs would eat even Jezebel's relatives because the Bible records that she was evil. Both the good man Naboth and the family of Jezebel who was evil were linked to being eaten by dogs. Surely there is a lesson to be learnt from this. Perhaps those preachers needed to go deeper into the WORD in order to know that the scriptures have come to pass. The Bible always fulfills its purpose.

PART THREE

CHAPTER SIX.

THERE IS POWER IN THE BLOOD OF JESUS.

We returned to England

My husband and I agreed to return to England after we had agreed to cancel the divorce, hoping to make our marriage work. There is nothing that God can not do to those who call on the name of Jesus. I was happy to start life afresh. I hoped to put the sad memories behind me. I was looking forward to serving the Lord. Having two education degrees from the University of Birmingham and two teaching qualifications from South Africa gave me hope to be employed as a schoolteacher. However that wasn't the case.

We arrived at the airport safely. We were talking, although coldly. We stayed at Nancy's house. I can remember my husband saying, "I still love you." Thank you Lord that was enough for me. Three days after wards I discovered that he had returned to Namibia. He had visited my mother-in-law and he left from there. He never even said, "good bye" to us. I cried as this hurt me very much.

I phoned him to find out the reason. He said it was "because we did not have our home back." He said he was very sorry. We kept in touch but it was becoming too much expensive, so we reduced the pace. I became very strong in the Lord and found a Pentecostal church in which to worship. Pentecostal churches are the churches that have the grace to operate according to the orders Jesus gave to his disciples:

"Do not leave Jerusalem, but wait for the gift I told you about, the gift my Father promised, John babtized with water, but in a few days you will be baptized with the Holy Spirit." **(The Acts 1:4-5)**

Jesus continued:

"But when the Holy Spirit comes upon you, you will be filled with power, and you will be witnesses for me in Jerusalem, in all Judea and Samaria, and to the ends of the earth." **(The Acts 1:8)**

These were the last instructions Jesus gave to His disciples before He was taken up to heaven. I always trusted God for our family. I knew that there was a teaching vacant post at our daughter's school so I applied and was short-listed for an interview. I was a strong candidate but another teacher, whose husband worked for the church got the post. I understood this, and I was instead appointed for another post that was to become vacant shortly afterwards. In the mean time I was happy to work within the school as a dinner lady.

From School Teacher to dinner lady

I enjoyed interacting with children again, although in a different role. Sometimes I did voluntary work, assisting the teacher in the classroom. There was another vacancy in the kitchen for about 25 pounds a week. I applied and got it despite the fact that I lacked experience in that area. In fact I was surprised to learn that a certain qualification was required in order to work in the kitchen.

Kitchen assistant

This was very hard, having to wash over 100 plates within a limited time. The only kitchen I was familiar with was my small kitchen at home, which was big enough to cook for 1-3 people. When washing up the water would spill all over me. Our supervisor would whisper "Pick up your speed as much as you can, I have to send a report which confirms your suitability in the job." I was very hurt and I started to suffer emotionally. Bells communicated a different message than usual. I spent most of the time crying when I got home. At the same time I did any work that came up.

A certain lady needed somebody to iron her clothes for five pounds an hour. I did two hours and went home with ten pounds. This was the same work I used to employ people to do for me in Africa. Now I had to do it myself. What a sliding scale! But one thing I never did was to doubt the presence of God. I just had to pray right. I pleaded for mercy for many days. Then I got another job as an office cleaner in the evenings.

Office-Cleaner

When workers were leaving the offices, I was always there putting on my apron. This was better, I didn't have to talk to anybody or work along a supervisor. It was just my vacuum cleaner, my dustcloth and I. I didn't have a toilet to clean, like in my previous work. I did my work sincerely, but I couldn't understand how life had turned to be like this.

I thought about my parents often and I kept asking myself why did my mum do those things to me? I knew that I had forgiven her, but it still hurt me very much. I lost trust in people, but I loved them more than I did before. My faith became very strong. One day the phone rang. My registration as a supply teacher had come through. I resigned both jobs and I got my career back.

Supply teacher.

I soon understood the job description of a supply teacher. I had been a full-time classroom teacher since 1980. There wasn't much difference, but I missed seeing the success of the children, I didn't have that opportunity until I got a long-term contract, which enabled me to teach in one school for a year. During this time the school was inspected. Good news! I passed the OFSTED inspection!

The manifestations of demons in Birmingham

Everywhere I went demons harassed me at night. While I was sleeping, I would see something, an insect or a spider and would jump to hit it. Many times I hit the wall very hard and my hand would be sore. Sometimes, I would be strong enough to shout, "Jesus" and then go to sleep again. As we were at my chief brides-maids' house; I explained to her what had happened, but assured her that I was free.

We moved to our own flat, but the nighttime problems continued. As I loved the Lord, I continued worshipping in another Pentecostal church. I gave testimonies about how the Lord had set me free from the demons. I still had the jerking movements. One day, one of the elders asked me about baptism. I told him that

I was baptised and he asked me on whose name. I referred him to **Matthew 28:19**. He explained that there is no other name by which we can be saved, and referred me to **Acts 2:38** Peter said to them;

"Each one of you must turn away from your sins and
Be baptised in the name of Jesus Christ, so that your
Sins will be for given; and you will receive God's gift
The Holy Spirit."

He felt I had to be rebaptised. I prayed about this, and agreed because I knew of the power in the name of Jesus.

My second baptism by full immersion

I agreed to go with the pastor and his wife to London, where a

Convention was being held in Lewisham. We went to the church that Sunday morning and the pool was prepared. I went into the pool with a sense of excitement about what the Lord would show me or give me after the baptism by full immersion. After I had said what I believed in, the Pastor said, "Zola I baptise you in the name of Jesus," and put me under the water.

The manifestation of demons in London.

As I came back onto my feet I jumped up and shouted, "oha-ha-ha-ha." These were same manifestations experienced in Namibia. I wanted to run away but they held me. They changed my clothes and then I managed to get loose. I ran to the road, at that time I wanted the cars to run over me. They caught me and took me to the school where the convention was being held. As we were approaching I saw flames of fire there and I cried. They put me into a room on my own. Two men, who were brothers in Christ, entered the room. One was from Nigeria and they clearly knew what they were doing as they were driving out the demons in the name of Jesus.

When they asked the name of the demon, it said it was Amar. They commanded Amar to go out in the name of Jesus. It refused saying it was locked in. I saw a vision of big, rusty, padlocks. The keys of the padlocks were in my mum's coffin and one of my relatives was keeping the keys of the coffin. I remembered seeing her lock the coffin and take the key before we went to the cemetery. None of the people who were ministering to me paid any attention when I told them about this revelation.

My new Pastor and his wife never made any attempt to help drive out the demon, it was left to the two brothers. These brothers tried, but perhaps they had other things to attend to and at times they left me there with the Pastor's wife looking after me. I just wanted to die. I was very hurt when the people got tired of driving the spirits out and deserted me, or when they just believed I was free when in fact this wasn't yet the case.

They came back and tortured the demon with the Word of God. When they put the Bible on my tummy, I cried as it burned me! The demon spoke loudly; calling out to other spirits including a spirit of tiredness. It was also praising Satan. Those who were around me left one by one. The Pastor's wife commented, that perhaps I had been sent by the Devil to destroy the work they were doing in the church. This comment hurt me very much, because I was suffering as a result of the Devil's activities myself, and I desperately needed their help. She never apologised to me.

Sister, I have forgiven you, because you told me that it was your first experience of seeing a person who was demon possessed. We have to remember that in the Ministry of Jesus Christ, all those who followed Him cast out the demons from those who were bound. Today's followers should realise that nothing has changed some Christians could be bound and they go in and out of church. They want to see the power of Jesus Christ in their lives, just like me. To you, those people who have been trusting God for breakthrough in certain areas of your lives, you have waited long enough, my advise to you is this.

Look around in your area, there may be a few churches that hate demons and are prepared to cast them out whenever they interfere in the life of their brethren. When evil spirits are interfering in someone's life, things just don't work out for this person. They need to have the demons cast out of them, then there's a release. We returned to Birmingham, but I knew that I was not free. I thank God for the sister in Christ, who comforted me, bought me a new hat and gave me a suit. I have not forgotten you. May the God we serve provide for all your needs?

The harassment was too much to endure

One night as I was sleeping, I saw an insect above my head so I hit it, but I actually hit the radio alarm which fell on the floor, I got up and regained my consciousness as I was jumping on it, it broke into pieces. This spiritual harassment continued.

The worst incident happened when I was sleeping, at about 10pm one night. Our daughter was watching TV. I saw an insect and I jumped up to hit it, but I actually hit her very hard on her left side of her face. This hurt me very much. I went to see another sister in Christ and she told me about a pastor, who had a church at Ladywood Community Centre. I agreed to visit the church.

I visited the sister who housed us when we were homeless; she was not born again at that time, I told her where I intended to go. As I mentioned this Pastor's name the demons manifested. I screamed and ran in the direction of the bedroom. I saw a vision of beads and shouted, "these beads" I ran back to the kitchen where she was standing. She tried to comfort me by patting me calling me by my surname, which is actually my ancestors' name. I cried, telling her to stop calling that name as it had a negative effect on me. I began to calm down. She was very scared.

We went to the church at Ladywood Community centre. It was in the evening, the Pastor made an altar call. I stood up, and started screaming and jumping trying to free my self as they were holding me. When I came to the front, the Pastor hit me very hard on the face and I fell down. I guess fear gripped him and thought I would attack him! Yes, sometimes this happened. The place where the church met was rented and everybody had to be out at 10pm so we had to leave. The pastor and his wife came to see me at home. He knew what do. He told me to say these words after him: "I renounce the ancestral spirits in the name of Jesus."

After saying the word "spirits", I couldn't go any further, my jaws clenched and all I could say was "wa-wa- wa." I couldn't say "in the name of Jesus." I heard his wife, who is English praying and interceding for me. I thank God for these people, please continue to cast out the evil spirits in your Ministry, even though it is not as easy as teaching the Word, you are following in the footsteps of Jesus and He will equip and strengthen you. It was about 3. 00 pm; they had to leave as they had to collect their children from school. I had to collect ours too. They left me panting hopelessly on the settee. They left the note that said: *"If the Son sets you free, then you will be really free indeed."* **(John 8: 36 Good News Bible)**

This was a powerful word from God. I did not need a prayer or a spoken word of faith that time. I needed someone to send fire from Heaven to burn the evil spirits until they surrendered, so that I could be free. No one was available to do that in Birmingham. I wrote a letter to Pastor Katie and told her that the demons were harassing me. She wrote back, commanding the spirits to leave me.

She asked me to arrange to visit her or for her to come to me. I knew that I needed prayer warriors, who would be willing to sacrifice their lives for the sake of my deliverance. In Britain I did not know any one.

I arranged to go to Pastor Katie in Malawi. The involuntary jerking movements were severe. Even when I was lying quietly, waiting on the Lord my legs would kick. My body would ache afterwards. I phoned her, and she told me that the church was fasting and praying for me. I was safe I just had to go.

The manifestation of demons in Malawi

Look what the Lord had done

One of the brothers in Christ offered their house for the prayer gathering. When we arrived there, other church members were already praying. I was sitting in the middle and they were surrounding me. I felt very weak. This time the demons were calling for two of my relatives. They obviously knew that my mum was dead. Pastor Katie spoke to them and she said, "go back, I want to talk to Zola." Everybody was involved, and they put Holy Spirit pressure on the demons. After refusing to come out, and claiming to be my husband, a voice came out of me and said, "break the umbilical cord." The brothers and sisters commanded the umbilical cord to be broken in the name of Jesus. By now it was early morning, my brothers and sisters in Christ were tired and everybody fell asleep.

On the second night they continued. I can still remember them shouting in their language that I didn't understand, "Tuluka, mudhina, ka

Jesu" (this meant, come out in the name of Jesus).

Pastor Katie was crying and begging God to complete this work. They took turns in driving the demons out, there was no break. Early the next morning a demon told them that I had many spirits in me, and I started to demonstrate this by imitating the cries of animals such as birds, snakes, cats and also dead people. As I did this, the praying team commanded them to come out in the name of Jesus. The full details of what happened are given below from the team that was involved in this deliverance.

Permission has been obtained from the writer to publish details of this letter.

Preparing for her deliverance, the Evangelism Team held overnight prayers. In addition, the Team agreed to be on fasting prayers until Zola was set free. On the eve of Tuesday 18th August 1998, the pastor told the Team that Zola had arrived and was at her house. The members available went to the house to see her and she said, "Praise the Lord" as she welcomed us.

The Pastor introduced the Team to Zola and a brother on behalf of the Team welcomed Zola. He assured her of her deliverance. He said she had arrived at the right time, at the right place and that the desire of her heart which was to be delivered from evil spirits was going to be met.

Upon hearing this, the demons, that were in her forced her to say, "NO!" while shaking her head in disagreement, as she turned her face away from us in hiding. This manifestation of demons did not shake us at all. We just trusted the Lord knowing that He is able. We met the following evening at Mr and Mrs Brown residence for the deliverance prayers.

Pastor Katie later led Zola into prayer to renounce the covenants that were made on her life. This was followed with serious manifestations of demons that were in her. Each one of us had a turn in commanding the demons to come out of Zola. A midst the commands, the demons uttered different sorts of discourging statements, "who are you? Shut up! We will kill you! We will sort you out! You are trouble makers!" All these words were said in fury as was evidenced by the wrinkles, which suddenly developed on the sister's forehead.

With determination, we continued praying for Zola's deliverance and we saw the demons beginning to succumb to the pressure of the fire of the Holy Spirit, who we were calling upon in the name of the Lord Jesus Christ. They came out one after another in a dramatic way, as they resembled different forms, which are: A Snake: She fell down and crawled on her belly with her tongue sticking out of her mouth just like that of a mamba.

The spirit of witchcraft: Zola flapped her arms pretended to fly.

The spirit of death: Zola ceased to breathe amd lay down like a corpse.

A hyena: She moved for a while in an exact manner as a hyena.

A frog: She hoped like a frog.

A fox: She flew on us as a wild fox.

A swine: She produced a sound as that of angry pigs.

A peacock or pride: She moved with mincing steps.

A mamaid: She pretended to swim in a way a fish does.

Gossip: She whispered as of she was despising and denouncing somebody.

Idolatry: She pretended to worship as if she held something in her hands.

A cat: She was mewing exactly in a way a cat does.

A leopard: She produced a sound like that of an angry leopard.

A lion: She charged like a roaring lion.

A tortoise: She was hiding her face as a tortoise does. When the listed spirits had come out, there was silence and we therefore asked if more remained.

In reply, one spirit identifying itself as "the commander" said it was still there. It claimed to be Zola's husband, and further told us that their marriage was officiated by Zola's mother when she was three. Inspite of our persistence the commander said it would not come out because it was locked in Zola's body with seven padlocks, which had been hidden in the pink coffin of Zola's mother at the cemetry, whose keys were kept by one of the relatives.

We ordered "the commander" to collect the keys from her, but it said she was hiding in the hills and would therefore come out the following day. Since it was already morning, we had to break and prepare for work.

The following night we convened again at the same place. In the name of Jesus we ordered "the commander" to come out of Zola. "Yes I will come out but I am taking my time", the demon said. Where should I go? To the graveyard we replied. "I don't stay in dead women, give me one of the women", it requested. No go to....we commanded. She is useless and I will kill her. "Guys we are in trouble", the demon shouted.

Zola screamed and after asking her the reason for her screaming she said that she saw Jesus looking straight at her. "Where is He?" We asked. "Right behind you" That was the demon's reply. There after the "commander" said, "Yes, I am coming out, Zola is no more my wife." Come out then, we commanded. "Yes but not now, because

I can not leave my things that are here," it said as she pointed at the navel. "Come out together with your meat at once, we charged." "Yes...break the umbilical cord." We did not give it time to rest but we commanded it to come out with the meat and break the umbilical cord where their covenant was. The demon responded to the command...She felt like the meat was stuck in the throat.

I felt nauseous and they gave me a dish. I wanted to vomit, but there was nothing in my tummy as I was fasting. I drank some water and this enabled me to vomit. As the water was clean I saw traces of blood, although not as clearly as in Namibia. Everybody glorified the Lord for what He had done. I believed that I was free and confessed it.

There is Power in confessing what you believe. This may seem a difficult thing to do for the 'quiet dignified born again Christians'. But who will shout for victory for you if you don't do it yourself? There is no school for learning to shout out to proclaim your victory.

Try closing your eyes when you are in church, and shouting loudly to the top of your voice. See if God our Father will not be merciful towards you and give you what you want. This is one of the weapons we possess to enable us to overcome. I have never seen a celebration or expression of joy done quietly. Have you? Even footballers will physically show their feelings when they score a goal. What about us, who are enemies of the forces of darkness? Surely, we should confess loudly and cheerfully the things we hope for **(Mark 11:22-24).**

CHAPTER SEVEN

OH NO, NOT AGAIN!

Another sister in Christ, who had been praying with me in our home, brought a leaflet about the Gilbert Deya Ministries crusade in Birmingham. I kept it without any thoughts. The 24th April 2001, arrived, this was the start of the crusade. That evening, I confidently decided to attend. As the ministers were greeting the congregation and introducing themselves, I knew the Lord had heard my cry to Him, asking Him to raise a committed army who would fight the forces of darkness in Birmingham.

I was blessed from the very first day, as the minister did not try to cover up the agents of the Devil, the witches and sorceress'. I felt the presence of Almighty God in the hall. Towards the end of the service, it was announced that there would be a deliverance service at 10 am every morning. My thoughts were, 'I am free, I don't need deliverance anymore'. I was wrong some evil spirits were still hiding in my body. Nor wonder my husband was unable to return to us. I didn't know, but the Lord knew.

Archbishop, Gilbert Deya preached from this passage.

Genesis 4: 1-16. When Cain killed Abel. God said, *"Why have you done this terrible thing? Your brother's blood is crying out to me from the ground, like a voice crying for revenge. You are placed under a curse and can no longer farm the soil. It has soaked up your brother's blood as if it had opened its mouth to receive it when you killed him. If you grow crops, the soil will not produce anything, you will be a* *homeless wanderer on earth.." (verses 10-12)*

As I raised my hands, I knew that I was not any different from a wanderer. I remembered the vision I had had when I was in Namibia, in which I had seen my late mum. I heard the question; "Do you remember when your mum admitted killing …?" Whether I was hearing my own mind or whether this was God speaking, I can't tell. I answered, "yes". Another question, "Who else died in you family and how?" I remembered, those who died in our family. I knew my late mum had admitted killing people, but I did not know how many or who were others.

At the time of a cousin's burial some relatives had begun to question the number of deaths in the family. They realised that the deaths were very frequent and the circumstances were often strange, they did not occur through sickness. The family held a ritual, asking God to intervene. Animals were slaughtered and a church service was conducted. Was this another form of blood sacrifice?

I knew that I needed to go for deliverance from the generational curses of my family. I also knew that I didn't have in-depth knowledge of my husband's family, however, judging from the behaviour of my husband, my father-in-law, who got divorced twice and my mother-in-law, something was obviously seriously spiritually wrong in their family too. My mother-in-law was divorced, and her son was having unhappy marriage. I went to stand in the gap for these families. Then I attended a special deliverance service.

After being given the time to speak to God about the presumed deeds, the Minister led us to attack the enemy. I was held at the back of my neck. I cried like a goat, loudly, then I jumped and began to fight, staring at those around me. The demons manifested again. As I was looking at a sister who was holding me with an aggressive face, somebody hit me very hard on my fore -head.

I fell on the floor with full force. They held me on the floor, pinning me with both arms. I felt nauseous and had the feeling to push like when someone is vomiting. Then suddenly I got up, totally surprised, and I knew that those demons were gone.

I felt very happy afterwards because it became clear to me that there was a good reason for me to suffer in the way that I had. I remembered how my Lord had suffered before He went to live with my Father in heaven. I rejoiced, and gave a testimony of my deliverance, against generation curses, the area that previously, had not been dealt with.

Today is the 14th May 2001

Deliverance by the fire of the Holy Ghost

The service by the Gilbert Deya Ministries resumed on Friday the 11th of May 2001. I encouraged our daughter to come with me. She had to come! Many ministers took part in the service. Pastor Amos, the son of Archbishop delivered the main Word. He pointed to certain people that had to go to the front, and stressed that this was not for sickness. I went to the front with joy. We had to breathe in and out. I was slain by the power of God. As I laid on the floor, I felt the manifestation of the demons, on my feet. I kept stretching my feet involuntarily.

Then my lower body began to move up and down. It wasn't long before the same loud cry of a demon came out of my mouth. There were no tears coming out but the voice screamed loudly calling my mum. The cry continued for some time, then it stopped. I laid there for a little while.

Somebody tapped me, and I got up. What an embarrassment! Our daughter was sitting on a chair on the front row looking at me. I felt a terrible pain inside me.

Lord why should I go through this again, I thought! Haven't you taught enough people about demons? "Mum are you alright," our daughter asked. I assured her that I was fine. I knew that the Lord was working on me. After the meeting I gave some ladies a lift home. I told them that I know the Lord loves me; I can go through this suffering as He did.

When I returned home, I tried to sleep, I felt a throbbing sensation on my left finger, the wedding ring finger. I had never taken my wedding and engagement rings off my finger since I'd dug them out of the ground in Namibia. I knew that this was another area that had been bewitched, so that my husband would forget about our marriage. I knew that this was a spiritual operation. Jessie phoned to ask how we were? I said to her, The same manifestations left me on the floor again, another show.

Our daughter was sitting in the first row and saw everything. "Only God himself can deliver me, this is not the work of man." She assured me, "it is finished" and advised me to talk to Pastor Amos about it. "But it is finished', she repeated."

On Sunday morning we went to church again. At the end of the service I asked a Prophet, what I could do about this demon? He said that I must fast for three days, then I should come to see him. I went home asking the Lord to anoint me with the Power to destroy all the work of the Devil. I felt the holy anger from within rise up in me. I confessed, "I will pursue you Devil, for the glory of my Lord Jesus Christ." I was actually doing all I could. Perhaps it was not enough.

Later, we were in the evening service Pastor Amos ministered about "living under a closed heaven." He explained how curses can block people from receiving from God, and called those who knew that they were affected, to come forward. The Holy Spirit said in my ear, "Go, your parents cursed you, remember, your mum never wanted you to get married, and you did."

When your dad asked your husband to pay a dowry, you refused. He asked you if "this man" was using your money, and you defended him. Your dad said "they (meaning men) use you and then abandon you, he must pay. Your parents cursed you." I jumped up and went to the front to have that curse broken.

I received from the Lord and I fell down, and lay on the floor for a while, I felt a deep sense of peace within me. I knew that I was free! I then received the anointing to resist the work of the enemy. I was on the floor again. When I got up I praised the Lord for setting me free from the demons. I had lived for thirty-seven years with evil Spirits inside my body and within four years the, Lord Jesus Christ of Nazareth had set me free. Truly our God is powerful, and there is nothing that he can not do!

The war against the spiritual forces of darkness continues

My love for God grew bigger. I was so grateful that He had revealed that some evil Spirits were still hiding inside me, it was no wonder that my husband was still distanced from us.

The truth was that evil spirits were still at work. I realised that my life was in a mess. I realised that no human being could help me in this situation. I needed the favour of God. I had to continue to serve Him with all my heart and mind and strength. I had to give all that I have to His Kingdom, my time, my physical strength, my money, and my heart. I made up my mind, not to miss any services. I worked as a school teacher full time and had a responsibility to look after our daughter properly in the absence of my husband.

However, that did not hinder me from working as an usher in the house of God. No situation prevented me from doing all these duties faithfully. When I was tired, I went to church. When I was not feeling very well, I went to the services. Once I couldn't speak because of stitches in my gums, I still went to the house of God. I knew the truth. God is looking at me all the time. He can see me all day; He even knows my thoughts.

Therefore I have no reason not to be in His presence, I feel safe in the presence of God. God has shown me many things in the Spirit. I know the truth about Him. I have seen His power several times. I have seen Him alive. I know He is really alive and wherever I am, He is there. I cannot cheat Him. Therefore my commitment is founded on evidence and experience, unlike a believer who is in church because he believes, but has not seen or experienced. I believed, testified and thanked God for this breakthrough.

It is written; *"Without faith it is impossible to please God, for he that cometh to God must believe that he is a rewarder of them that diligently seek him."*
(KJV Hebrews 12:6)

My life style continued to change. I made more and more commitment to the work of God. Many times I asked myself many questions, "Why did mum get involved with Satan?" How did she get involved? Why did mum give me to the demons? Many times I answered myself. "God has chosen me. He loves me. He had a purpose to allow me to be conceived in the womb of a witch. He had a purpose to allow me to suck milk from the breasts of a witch. He had a purpose to allow David to move away from us."

Jesus had to delay his visit to Lazarus. Lazarus had to die and lie in the grave for four days. This was the plan of God so that *"the Son of God might be glorified thereby."* **(John 11:4)**

If I had not suffered what I did, no one would have known about the witchcraft activities that my mum and other relatives were involved in. If God by His mighty power had not shown me the source of my miseries, they would have never been found out, and my mum would probably still be alive doing more evil.

I was determined to press on in this Spiritual struggle, not only in my own territory, but also on behalf of the nations at large. I knew the strategies that Satan uses to attack people. I knew that I am a living testimony and I wanted everybody to know that our God is powerful. I knew the tricks of the demons; I could see demons manifesting in people in church. I shared the feelings of other believers who were still bound and I wanted to aid them in the fight against the devil and his agents. I knew that these evil forces had no power when the army of God was up in arms to destroy them, and then they would surrender easily. Little did I know that some demons were not gone yet, but God knew.

On 9th November 2001, just before the end of the service, Pastor Robert from Los Angeles broke down, he shared, "God is showing me, there is a woman here, your marriage is attacked, terribly, terribly…" Before he had finished, I jumped up and down with both feet and forced myself towards the front row where the other pastors were sitting. I couldn't stop myself from pushing the people who were trying to hold me back. I did not scream as I used to and I ended up on the floor. I knew the demons that were commissioned to destroy my marriage were still hiding in my body. In faith I knew that I would be free. I knew that Jesus would complete the work that He had started, and He certainly did at the end!

My faith was strong, but I was still amazed at what had taken place. I went home not saying very much. I made a commitment to God, "Lord if this is your will, to demonstrate your power to the nations, let it be. With Jesus, your Son, it was not easy, but He had a mission to fulfil. So let it be." I never cried, I worshiped God and fell asleep, in our lighted bedroom. Ever since February 1997 I have not switched our bedroom light off at night.

The next Saturday morning

I was lying on our bed, it was around 8 am. I opened my eyes and said, "My Father in Heaven, good morning, I love you. Thank you for loving me. Father shall I pray or worship you?" I began to thank Him for showing me what no human being could see. I thanked Him for setting me free from these invisible enemies that had not only nearly destroyed my marriage, but many other marriages too. I knew that from now on, whenever He chose to reveal these enemies to me, as soldier of Jesus Christ I would wage a "defensive war against them."

I asked the Lord not to allow me to

be hurt this time. Many times brethren had hurt me; some had taken revenge because I'd hit them while under the control of the evil spirits. Some I guess, lacked understanding that at that moment I was not myself, although I was able to hear and see everything that was happening.

As I lay there I began to worship God. My eyes were shut, and I saw a vision of the three pastors standing before me, as in the previous night's service. Immediately the demons in me manifested. As I was lying on my back, I kicked my legs and shook both arms rapidly. I grabbed the handkerchief that I had been given as a point of contact for prayer. I commanded the demons to come out of my body. I declared that my body is the temple of God. At that time I declared to God that this was my final day of deliverance.

I heard a voice that said, "phone the pastors." I knew they were out but the voice insisted, "phone." I phoned and sister Bahati answered. I told her what happened. She said, "let's pray." She began to command the demons to come out. I jumped up and down, until the receiver fell down. I fell on the settee. I screamed calling out for my mum and other two relatives. "We killed her," said the demons. They spoke again," who are these? We don't know them. They are powerful." They repeated this. I tried to get up and couldn't, I wanted to reach the phone. My hand began to shake. I could hear the sister praying. She was very powerful and she was able to send fire through the phone. I had a burning sensation in my tummy. I was crying rolling all over the floor.

Our daughter came into the living room and spoke on the phone. I couldn't speak, I tried but my jaws were stiff. Again I had a very strong thought that said, "Go to the pastors, and do not leave until they have finished the work."

The phone rang and it was one of my sisters in Christ. I just cried and she said, "bring the child." I took the handkerchief, held it in my hand and called, "Jesus." I drove to her house with our daughter, calling on Jesus until I reached there. I left her and drove to the Pastor's house. Sister Bahati continued to drive the demons out. She became very tired, and there was no sign of departure.

When the Pastors arrived, Pastor Amos called, "sister, Zola" the demons showed themselves by kicks and rapid jerks. I tried to answer, but all was in vain. I only could say, "shja-shja-shja." They left me for a while and when they returned Pastor Daniel called me. I shook my head for "no". He held my hand up and guided me up the stairs.

I sat down and the spiritual warfare began. I remember lying on the floor, the demons called, "Lucifer, war." I tried to fight against the Pastors. But it was not I; I would never have such power and strength to break through three strong men. Thank you Jesus, none of them hit me in retaliation or hurt me. The demons surrendered, the Pastors were very powerful. They drove them out. I continued to confess my freedom, and truly I knew that Jesus has set me free. I was very tired and I drove back home. Thank you Lord Jesus.

God has showed me His power and love for human kind. Now I know, that Satan exists and he has agents, which he sends to do his evil deeds. However, if people choose to pretend that these forces don't exist, surely they are in a position of suffering and are not doing anything about it. My message to you reader is this; when you come to Jesus, seriously, He is able to reveal these mysteries, and not only reveal them, but deal with them effectively. He is alive!

A few weeks passed, I was happy internally and I continued to confess that I am free. I knew that God would confirm His word. I knew that when I was free from the demon of marriage destruction, my husband would say, "my wife, I'm sorry, I love you." That was the message I had last heard seven years ago.

My husband had always assured me of his love and I knew he was not lying. I trust him, until this day. I know that husband is mine until "death do us part." The joy of the Lord was, and always is, my strength. Our daughter and I waited patiently for the doorbell to ring. I knew that my husband would spend Christmas 2001 with us.

As I was praying in the service one evening. I realised that I had kept some divorce letters. These papers were in our flat. I had cancelled and nullified the whole of the Devil's plot in the spirit realm.

But when the scripture in **James 2:26,** *"Faith without action is dead."* was spoken in that service, I realised that I had to act on those letters.

When I got home I found the letters and I cut them up with scissors and just left the pieces to show the evidence of the power of God. The only complete document I kept was our marriage certificate. I believed that the divorce proceedings were cancelled in the natural realms, as well as in the spiritual realms, and our marriage was well and truly ALIVE!

Pastor Robert is back.

A few weeks passed by and Pastor Robert revisited the church. This time he was going to take control of the church in the absence of Pastor Amos. Pastor Amos encouraged the congregation to see him for counselling. One day, I heard a silent voice, "phone, and go to see the pastor." Take the destroyed documents and your live marriage proof with you.

When two witnesses agree on something, it shall come to pass. I did exactly that and he was able to see me straight away. He asked me what I wanted God to do for me. "Speak life into our marriage, I want my husband back, I will keep to my vows", I replied. "You will get what you want", he confirmed. We held onto the marriage certificate and he prayed. As he stood up and laid his hands on me in prayer the demons manifested.

Another painful lesson began. He drove them out with authority. It was a silent war, but a very powerful one. The demons were overpowered. One spoke and claimed to be "too big" to come out through any of the possible openings. In the name of Jesus, he commanded it to break. Immediately I felt the breaking and scattering in my tummy, it made noise as when one has an upset stomach. The fire of the Holy Spirit was so great that another one, or maybe the same one, shouted in anger, "she will never make it." For those people who claim not to believe that demons are real, I testify that the voices all came from my mouth but spoke in the third person "she", meaning me. It became clear that the demon was responding to the confessions we usually make in church, "I will make it, in the name of Jesus."

When demons are in someone's body, those people walk in and out of the church with them. They listen to everything concerning that person's life and when that person speaks, or make plans the demons listen and plot how to stop them and attack successfully. Christians, keep quiet, speak about the news and the plans of the Kingdom that glorifies God, the Devils cannot stop those.

Pastor Robert continued to put fire on the demons inside me, commanding them to go out, in the name of Jesus. I was jerking and rolling on the floor, but not screaming as at previous times. He discerned the evil spirit of death and hell and commanded it to go. It manifested. I actually fell on my back; lay stiff withheld my breath as if I was dead. I heard him saying, "you will not kill her." On previous occasion the demons had confessed that I do not die, they have tried to kill me several times. It is true that I have narrowly escape with my life many times.

As the demons were departing one of them looked back swearing, it screamed, "we will come back." That was the last kick of a dying horse. There were sounds of many steps and I saw shadows moving in the same direction. My body ached for a week afterwards, from the involuntary jerking movements.

Jesus has taught us to forgive those who trespass against us. I have forgiven my mum and her team. However, they should repent, so that their sins can be forgiven or else…

Many people, including Christians who are born again and Spirit filled in this world could be possessed by the demons, but they do not know. How do I know? The signs are evident. The occurrence of destruction, pain, singleness, divorce, barrenness, suicide and sexual immorality are all very high in today's society. To those people who would like to know the source of their suffering, I say this. If you have been attending your church for years and you have not experienced a miracle in those areas that are pressing in your life and if you are trusting God for an answer but the years are going by and nothing is happening, then stop wasting your time and money!

Find a church with ministers that are called of God, anointed and given many of the Spiritual gifts. These men and women of God will teach you about eternal life, but they will also help you to fight the forces of darkness that are oppressing and destroying you, while our Lord Jesus has not yet returned. They will not avoid the subject of demons and the need for deliverance.

To accept Jesus as your personal Saviour is the start of a successful life, however, demons do not always automatically flee, when someone accepts the Lord. Often to get them to leave the body that they have occupied for a long time requires war; "I mean serious war, with time." Demons have confessed many times that they need a human body to live in.

My experience has taught me that this area is not a joke. I have been born again for over five years now. I do not miss any church services including all night prayer meetings and I am a cheerful giver towards the work of God. I have worshipped God faithfully in a few churches that the Lord has sent me to.

It is by His mercy that in "only" two of these churches, has the Power of God been strong enough to trigger these demons to manifest. I thank God that on all those occasions, men and women of God put aside all of their personal and family obligations and engaged in a fight against the evil spirits. They risked their lives and families for my sake. They knew that Satan avenges, but for the sake of the gospel of Jesus Christ, they followed in His footsteps, to cast out the demons.

As I stated above, Christians can have demons, even ministers. Demons are organised in different contingents according to their tasks, for example, destruction through alcohol, fornication, adultery, poverty, tiredness, barrenness, rejection, decrease and dirt etc. When demons of alcoholism are in somebody's tummy, that person needs to drink. He or she is forced to get alcoholic drink into their mouth, even if there is no money available, they would even steal to get it, they have no control over their mind. The world refers to them as "alcoholics". Have you come across people like these? They are seen among us. My mum and her team of witches used these demons to destroy Rachel. I was very close to her and I will continue to mourn her death.

These demons came into me when I was three years old, so they can come into anybody at any time before they take God seriously. They have to be cast out in order to go, war has to be waged against them. Only the trained soldiers of Jesus Christ are able to engage in this type of war and fight effectively using various spiritual warfare strategies, which I will not reveal for the sake of the protection of the Kingdom of God.

If you have been sleeping, it's time to wake up. Not later but now, you can make it. All things are possible with God. Surely you want the good things in life; a happy marriage, a balanced home with everything prosperous, children who do well and find favour at school and good work of your choice.

You especially want these things, when you call yourself a Christian who gives physical and financial to the work of God. Sickness, diseases and many more attacks should not come near your home. I thank God for choosing me, and giving me this knowledge because without such, it could be difficult to understand the spiritual realm, as it is invisible to the normal eye. This is why we should strive for the supernatural eye in order to see. God can only grant the supernatural, and no man can give it without God. Now I can speak about the spiritual things I have seen.

A few days after the final deliverance session, I returned home from work to find the following message on the answer machine: *Yaah! This is my message I'm mn… I'm mn…. Sorry, I'm, Nikki's father* (pause) and I'm calling to talk to Nikki but her cell phone seems to…. The number I got seems not to work. So I'mn. Nikki I've been trying to call you. I just want to say "Nicky I love you" "I hope you get this message. Bye."

This was my husband's voice, thank you Jesus. He had come to his senses.

Free at last

I am free! Free from demonic oppression. Hallelujah! Thank you Jesus! Free at last! Thank you King of Kings! I shouted and jumped with joy as the clock ticked 23.57 on 31st

December 2001. Yes, I have victory over my enemies. There is victory in the blood of Jesus. So, what is next? God has provided my spiritual ground for training.

Captives have to be set free in the name of Jesus. Somebody has to go to the battle-front. I will avenge for Rachel. I declare war over the forces of darkness and their agents. We will pursue them until Jesus returns. I will go to war because I know God is in me. This is not the end, but just the beginning, watch out for the next publication.

CHAPTER 8

THERE IS NOTHING THAT THE LORD, JESUS CHRIST CANNOT DO

In this concluding chapter I have summarised the whole process that made me come out boldly and write this book based on my experience. I have seen God at work. I have proved the Bible. Today I am a living testimony having a very peaceful life serving God who has showed me that He really loves me. However, Satan is also real.

As he was at work from the time he was thrown out of heaven by God, so is he even now. Day and night, his work is to steal, kill and destroy people. I thank God that Jesus Christ of Nazareth came in order to destroy what the Devil has done. **(1 John 3:8 Good News Bible).** My mum gave birth to me and brought me up. Other people came to our home, ate food with us, I trusted them therefore told them everything about myself. They let us down. I did not know what was in their hearts. What a good lesson to learn? Did these people know what they were doing? I don't know.

Satan was evil from the beginning. He tricked my family and I through the witchdoctors. He denied me the peace I deserved. He abused me sexually, emotionally, physically, and financially. These areas of life cover all aspects of human life. Satan dominated all of these areas and I hate him and his agents. Many times I was in agony, the pain was at times too much to endure, to the extent that I didn't see the reason to live. For 26 years, I didn't know who was behind my suffering. God took me through various stages, which were very unpleasant and hard indeed:

Firstly: He revealed the demons

that were living in my body. Many people do not think that their problems may be caused by demons in them. Evil spirits are real, they are spirits; you can not see them. Whether they are in your body or not, it is impossible to know until you are in the powerful presents of God and God reveals them.

I also did not know that I was possessed, until the merciful God revealed this hidden truth. To be possessed meant that demons had taken total control of all my senses. What a life! I was unable to reason independently; somebody had to give me advice. Readers bewise, demons are real, they are the same as at the time of Jesus.

Secondly: God showed me in a vision *(I didn't know that it was a vision that time)* my family members who had directly carried out the evil activities that were destroying my life. Nobody would have managed to convince me that my mum was my physical destroyer, had it not been revealed to me supernaturally. If I had not seen them standing in front of me, and if Jill had not confirmed all their witchcraft activities, it would have been very difficult for me to believe their evil work and strive to get my victory. Christians, believers, we need to seek, so that we can know the truth. We should not rest until we get the hidden knowledge directly from God. There is a price to pay for freedom. However, it can bring joy in its fullness into your life, so surely it is worth pursuing. I have not yet met a faithful person who regrets drawing close to Jesus.

Jesus Christ really is alive. When we go through difficulties, He is looking, waiting for us to call on Him for help. If you want to prove this, just live according to His teachings, commit yourself to Him and ask Him to show up.

Satan also exists and is still at work; even today his kingdom is organised. He has his representatives that monitor everything; just like shadow ministers do in earthly governments. His network has good communication and he and his agents are sincere in their work, to kill, steal and destroy. His work is in operation 24 hours a day, 7 days a week, continuously.

You can't defend yourself against him until you take time to think and follow the pattern of your life. You can't fight him successfully until you take an in-depth study of him and his operations and how to weaken and bind him and his agents in war. This is the information that helped those who were around me to fight a successful war. We sought and found information that enabled us to direct our Spiritual weapons of war right at the targets. There is no point in shooting to miss, is there? You just get tired.

Thirdly: God fought for me. In the book of **Zachariah 4: 6,** God says, *"It is not by might nor by Power but by my Spirit."* **(King James Version)**. Good News Bible explains it clearer, *"You will succeed, not by military might, or by your own strength, but by my Spirit."* I succeeded by the Spirit of God. When both my mum and dad, whom I trusted, died. God, who was fighting for me, did not protect them against the enemy. God is our defender. However, their death was double, in that, dogs ate their bodies.

It is my prayer that as you read this book, you will take everything seriously. This is not a fairy tale or fiction. Draw closer to God, He will fight for you. Even your closest family will suffer the wrath of God, if they deserve it. The life of an orphan can also be different. Living a life of just wanting God around you; because you have lost trust in human beings completely is another topic on its own. I feel safe when I am in the presence of God and I am still working to get over of the feeling of being deceived by all the people I trusted, including my mum, the woman who gave birth to me.

Fourthly: The Lord Jesus Christ healed our daughter and I from a vaginal discharge that I'd had, for twenty nine years, and she had had since she was four months old. The demons admitted sexually abusing us and causing this infection. Doctors could not find anything wrong when they tested us; therefore there was no cure available. Now what a joy it is to stay dry all day! Women open your eyes, if you suffer in this way, it is not normal. Doctor Jesus is able to heal you. Can you imagine how I feel when I can stay dry all day long?

Fifthly: At last all the demons are gone! My husband has come back to us.

I told that woman who tried to destroy my home and marriage in order for her to have my husband, that he was mine. I said to her "He will never marry you! Ask God for your own husband!" And these words have materialised.

Why do women and men allow themselves to be used by the Devil to break up marriages? If they knew the pain that is caused when families are torn apart by the Devil, when children are suffering as a result of broken homes, surely they wouldn't choose to be part of these evil deeds. However, the tears that are shed never drop in vain. *"God will place cowards, traitors, perverts, murderers, the immoral, those who practise magic, those who worship idols, and all liars in the lake burning with fire and sulphur."* **(Revelations 21:8)**

Should men and women resist to be used this way, there would be no divorce. The evil spirits would not find any body to operate through.

The evil spirits were stubborn, but very weak. They did not want to leave my body, where they had made their home. The power that is in the name of Jesus drove them out. As it was at the time of Jesus, so it is even today. The blood of Jesus is powerful. Glory be to Jesus, our Lord.

Here below is my checklist for complete deliverance:
* I love people
* My husband is back to us
* No dreams having sexual intercourse with the men I know and those I don't know
* My fingers are set free and holy; I use them to hold things
* I don't jump up to hit the spiders and other insects at night
* I will never hit my husband while I'm sleeping again
* I will never hit our daughter in my sleep again

* I do not allow anger to occur in me
* I do not talk about myself to every body, only Jesus; I can keep secrets
* I have confidence in myself and, I don't have to check with anyone
* I am faithful to the Lord
* I have all I need
* I have peace and rest within me and I live to serve the Lord.
* I work voluntarily as an usher in the house of God in order for Jesus to be glorified through all the earth.

Finally: If I had hardened my heart when I heard about Jesus, where would I be now? How would this truth be known? Maybe my mum, the woman I trusted, who gave me to the demons, and my dad, who I loved, would still be alive. But the fact is this; I would not be free! I would still trust family and other people and not Jesus. Yes, my maiden family betrayed me! Yes, a family can let you down. Where does this lead us? Our families need Jesus, and then the enemy will not use them against us. I love my family…despite…I have not seen or heard of them for the last five years. I miss Tim, wherever you are, I have not forgotten you, "I love you Tim!"

This is how it started, I said, *"Lord Jesus, forgive me all my sins, I believe you are the Son of the living God. You died, rose, and you are coming back to judge the world. Come into my heart, Amen."*

Readers, should you realise that things are not going on well with you, do not waste time, try Jesus. Look for a Pentecostal church where signs, miracles and wonders are happening in the name of Jesus now. Just believe that Jesus Christ will take you out of the hard situation you are in. He did it for me. He will do it for you. I have not written this book to entertain you, but to let you know that you don't have to accept pain and troubles around you. There is a definite way to come out. May your deliverance begin now as you finish reading this book, in the mighty name of Jesus, *Amen?*

Afterword by Pastor Amos Deya

What a mighty God we a serve! He has proved to be faithful and just whenever we trust and call on him. This book has a dynamic effect to every reader. You shall be lifted, encouraged and strengthened in every struggle you are going through. God was so faithful to deliver the author of this book from every clutches of the enemy and I believe that every reader shall experience that divine intervention. As the bible says in **Exodus 14:14** *the Lord shall fight for you and you shall hold your peace.* Praise the Lord!

Book two

Authority over Satan

Introduction

I thank the Lord for being so good to my family.

When my daughter Jane's marriage was to take place in Oklahoma in the United States of America, My wife was privileged to travel to London from Kenya. I made the decision to introduce my wife, Mary to the congregation of the new church that had just been opened in Manchester, here in the United Kingdom.

The message in this book was given to me by the Lord while I was in Manchester.

Unique Grace

I believe that God has given us His grace. This grace is unique, and I can say that because not many persons have received this kind of grace from God. It is tangible; it is historical - the way in which God has used my wife in Kenya, here in London and in other nations abroad.

The Historical Miracle Birth

Mary Deya has been used by God to minister to Mr. and Mrs. Odera, in Kenya, a couple that was unable to have a child. Mrs. Odera had been pregnant before in 1984, but after (5) months the child disappeared from her womb. The gynaecologist and other doctors could not find the child in her womb and since that incident, she had not been able to conceive. Mrs. Odera was in the time of menopause for about 14 years when she received The first miracle baby. She had passed her fiftieth (50) birthday and they had both given up trying to get a baby.

Nevertheless, Mrs. Odera got pregnant in 1999 when my wife Mary Ministered to her in Nairobi, Kenya. My wife prophesied to her that she had a baby in her womb. Nine months later the first child was born. Mrs. Odera has given birth to eight babies within the

last three (3) years And is now pregnant
with their ninth child. These babies are
miracle babies! They are products of
the miraculous and powerful anointing
of God.

The doctors have advised her to do
an operation because it is getting out of
hand. My only concern is that the
husband is fifty-seven years old,
coming to his fifty-eight (58) birthday
very soon, and the wife is now fifty-
four (54) years old and they are both
unemployed.

There is no income support in
Kenya and they are not able to look
after the children on their own. My
wife and myself have been maintaining
them, since we saw that miracle. We
pay their rent, we contribute money
and make sure that they have food, and
clothing for the children. As long as we
live the children must eat and drink. We
do this because we know that the
miracle they have received is for God's

glory. There are a few persons in London, who have also given help to this couple. An ex-muslim and a lady from Guyana used to help, but they have now left the Ministry.

I want to encourage you ladies and gentlemen, we serve a living God and he Is able to do great things in your lives. My wife and I can claim to know God by the work that he has done to us. Some people do not see this as God's doing. Some even take it for a joke. Nine children being born in three (3) years is not a normal event. Do you know of any other woman, who has given birth like that in the world, with all the children alive and healthy?

It is a miracle!

We have never heard this type of story in the world before. Pussy-cats can give birth like that because they are animals, but according to human biology it takes nine months for a baby to be properly developed in the womb.

This miracle is above human understanding.

The Anointing Slaughtered Lives

When Moses was in the process of delivering God's people from the land of Pharaoh, he performed many impossible feats in the presence of Pharaoh, the Egyptians and the children of Isreal.

"Moses then said to the King, The Lord says 'At about midnight, I will go through Egypt, and every first-born son in Egypt will die, from the King's son, who is heir to the throne, to the son of the slave woman, who grinds grain. The first-born of all the cattle will die also." **Exodous 11:4-5-GNV.**

By the words that Moses spoke under the anointing of God, he caused people and cattle to be slaughtered. He told Pharaoh that if he refused to release God's people, the Israelites, the first-born boy child of the families in Egypt would die, also the first-born of all the cattle. Moses spoke words that brought murder. He killed by his words. He told Pharaoh that even his (the King's) own son would die. Moses spoke words that made the first-born male of human beings and the first-born of all cattle in the entire country to die. He murdered them by His words. He spoke and the frist-born of human beings, even cats, dogs and rats died.

The Untouchable Power

What power did Moses have?

Now, I want you to figure out how the water was turned to blood in The entire country, even in the wooden tubs and stone jars, when Moses Said so. How could Moses speak and flies swarm the country at his Command? How did the frogs come up and cover the land of Egypt, in the houses, the countryards and even on the King's table. I urge you to figure out how these miracles took place. God brought it to pass. By the power of God the impossible became possible!

The Israelites came out of Egypt and were going to Canaan, 'the Promised land' but the Egyptians were chasing them and they ended up at the Red Sea where they could not pass over to the other side. The Israelites realized that they could not go any further. They reached as far as they could go and their enemies were getting closer.

The bible says, *"Moses held out his hand over the sea, and the Lord drove the sea back with a strong east wind. It blew all night and turned the sea into dry land. The water was divided, and the Israelites went through the sea on dry ground, with walls of water on both sides."* **Exodus 14:21-22 GNV.**

Can science and the technology of humans explain how Moses by the Power of God divided the water in two? This is a miracle that has never been seen again since the time of Moses. Except that day that it was needed for God's people to escape from their enemies, it has never happened again. When things get tight, and you find that there is no way for you to pass, God can divide water into two for you to cross over.

The agony of Barrenness

Mr. and Mrs. Odera suffered rejection; they were abused and laughed at Because they were unable to have children. They lived without having even one child to make noise in their house. It is better to have a child in your house making noise, than not to have any at all. People can know that you are somebody who is blessed, and it brings comfort to every woman to have a child to nurse. Even if they are crying for sweets and hamburger and you do not have it. It is good to be a mother and a father to many children. The noise of your children laughing and talking in your home is a music that brings joy to every marriage.

Can you imagine that you grew up with your brothers and sisters and now you are elderly with your hair getting white and you are lonely; the two of you are in the house from the first day of your marriage without any children? It is so painful. Some people work, they make good money but they do not have any children to benefit from their labour and they live lonely and empty lives without the joy that children brings to a home.

In Africa, if a wife cannot give birth to children the family will force the husband to marry another woman, whether she likes it or not. The man will not have only one wife, if she cannot have at least six children. Forget about the pills and coils that woman are using here in Britain. The family in Africa must be more than two children or there is a problem. They do not have the spirit of 'stinginess' or 'poverty' that westerners have.

Even the highly educated in the western countries say that they cannot afford to give birth to too many children. They claim that they will not be able to look
after the children so they use birth control pills and coils. Some are managers, but they are mean. They do not want to share their lives and to spend money on children that they can produce from their own bodies. They do not know that God. loves children and will provide for the family. I see a bright future for the children of the Odera family.

The Illiteracy of Professionals

We are talking about miracles!

Jesus walked on water and we have been talking about this and every preacher, preaches about Jesus walking on water. Is there anyone else on earth that has ever walked on water? Is it easy to walk on water? He also ordered Peter to walk but he never made it without Jesus' help.

This is what proves that Jesus has the unique power to do what others cannot do. If you test archbishops, cardinals and even the pope by giving them water to walk on, they would sink. But Jesus walked on water. If you tell this to some people, they will abuse you, even professionals and university graduates. This is because they are illiterate to the things of miracle. Yes, you can be a graduate from the university of man and illiterate to the things of God. Miracles are above human understaning. It is good when you have already been laughed at. When people have rejected you and they have talked negative of you and treated you like rubbish in a dustbin - like the way they treated Mrs. Odera, a miracle from God will qualify you to be treated with respect.

Mrs. Odera had been to many places to seek help. She said she even went behind her husband's back to visit many witch-doctors to see if they could do something for her to have a baby. She went to every doctor and pastor that knew, and nothing came from her womb.

Folks, I believe that God knows where to send you to get the help that will bring him the glory. There are some places that God has His own people who He uses to uniquely prove himself to others, that He exists and that He is the all powerful, Almightly God!

For God to use you as His servant, it is costly to you. You have to be submitted Fully to God. It is not because my wife Mary is married to an archbishop that made her able to perform a miracle. That could not qualify her to be used by God to perform a miracle for Mr. Odera's wife. It is not because Mary's husband is 'born again'. There are many wives of pastors and bishops who cannot do this. She has to be empowered by God in order to do this.

We have heard of the wives of bishops, who killed themselves for different reasons. The wife of a bishop in our country hanged herself, on the church premises when she found out that her husband was having an affair.

He was having sex with another woman. You may not like when I say it like this, but I am not covering it up.

I will talk straight, a bishop was having sex with a secretary in the church and in a few years the woman gave birth to a child who looked just like the bishop. The child had the gap at the front teeth like the bishop. The child had the eyes, mouth, face and even the toes of the bishop. When the people started to question the business of the bishop, the wife killed herself. It is not always comfortable to be a bishop's wife. Unless you play your part in being a godly woman, God cannot show you His glory. The Glory on Men of God is Dangerous

We are living in a world of destruction, where some people are just talking but have nothing to prove that God is in existence. The same God that was with Moses, was with Elijah and Elisha. Elijah called down fire from

heaven to destroy the soldiers who were sent to arrest him. **2 Kings 1:10-13.** Elisha caused bears to Tear the children who were mocking him to pieces.
2 King 2:23-42.

I want to make a point here; when God loves His servant he can kill people because of that man. A servant of God is dangerous when he is under the anointing. This is what I want to let you know. Moses killed the first-born males of the Egyptians, including Pharaoh's son. Was Moses "born again?" Did he kill anyone?

Yes, they were people like you-men and woman, whose first-born died. This shows how dangerous Moses was as an anointed man of God. When God wants to deliver you, he will destroy even people, just to make sure that he does for his people what He wants to do. Somebody say "yes"

The Bible says in **1 Kings 17:1-4,** A Prophet named Elijah, from Tishbe in Gilead, said to King Ahab *"In the name of the Lord, the living God of Israel, whom I serve, I tell you that there will be no dew or rain for the next two or three years until I say so". Then the Lord said to Elijah, "Leave this place and go east and hide yourself near Cherith Brook, east of the Jordan. The brook will sullpy you with water to drink, and I have commanded ravens to bring you food there."*

Then man called Elijah, when he stopped the rain from falling because of the prophetic words he gave about the drought - the whole nation was hunting him because they wanted to kill him. People like yourself, not the trees nor the stones but people like yourself who breathe fresh air and walk on two legs. They came seeking Elijah to kill him.

In the book of **2 Kings 1:1-10** the Bible says after the death of King Ahab of Israel the country of Moab rebelled against Israel.

King Ahaziah of Israel fell of the balcony on the roof of his palace in Samaria and was seriously injured. So he sent some messengers to consult Baalzebub, the god of the Philistine city of Ekron, in order to find out whether or not he would recover. But an angel of the Lord commanded Elijah, the prophet from Tishbe, to go and meet the messengers of King Ahaziah and ask them, "Why are you going to consult Baalzebub, the God of Ekron? Is it because you think there is no God in Israel? Tell the King that the Lord says", You will not recover from your injuries; you will die! Elijah did as the Lord commanded, and the messengers returned to the King.

They amswered, "We were met by a man who told us to come back and tell you that the Lord says to you, 'Why are you sending messengers to consult Baalzebub, the god of Ekron? Is it because you think there is no god in

Israel? You will not recover from your injuries; you will die!"

"What did the man look like?" the King asked. He was wearing a cloak made of animal skins, tied with a leather belt," they answered. "It's Elijah!" the King exclaimed. Then he sent an officer with fifty men to get Elijah. The officer found him sitting on a hill and said to him, "Man of God, the King orders you to come down."

"If I am a man of God," Elijah answered, "may fire come down from heaven and kill you and your men!" At once fire came down and killed the officer and his men. We can just imagine that the fifty (50) soldiers may have looked like giants, big in body like your Pastor Mensah. They knew that Elijah was alone - one man, yet fifty men went to get him. Elijah must have seen them coming because he was sitting on a hill. The soldiers ordered him to come down. Elijah told God to send fire. That was not God's will; that was Elijah commanding God to do what he wanted. Elijah challenged God. He told God to prove that he Elijah was His servant by sending fire to kill the soldiers.

These men left their wives as widows and their children as orphans because the fire burnt them to death. We can imagine that there was no trace of the bodies after the fire. We call that cremation. There was no funeral. They were all burnt to death because of Elijah, a dangerous anointed man of God.

I Believe that Elijah and Elisha were like Pastor Mensah and myself. Folks, Mensah has got the mantle here in Manchester, and if you play with him you can be destroyed like the children who were torn into pieces by the bears.

The anointing that was on Elisha's life, caused the young children who were teasing him to be cursed by his words and they were utterly destroyed. Elisha did not care whether they were children, they called him 'baldy' and made fun of him. Elisha never cared whether their mothers would be left without children.

The Bible says, in **2 King 2:24.** *"Elisha turned around, glared at them, and cursed them in the name of the Lord. Then two she-bears came out of the woods and tore forty-two of the boys to pieces."*

Witches Kill Ignorant Christians

It is sad that most of the Christians today are so ignorant. They water down the words of the Lord. Your PhD. Degree has nothing to do with being able to call down fire from heavens. Somebody say 'witchcraft'!

We are in the western world where

there are several races of people living together. In Kenya we do not have many nationalities like you have it here. In Kenya we only have Kenyan witches, but here in England we have the British witches of Nigeria, the West Indies, India and Many other nations all living here.

I want to tell you that the power that is needed now is the power that was on Moses, Elijah and Apostle Paul. This is the power that is needed now in order to fight against the witches' power in these western countries that are making people to be single.

The devil knows very well that if you are not happy you cannot be next to God, and no one can be comfortable if they are single. If you are single and you want to get married you are not happy. You are chasing marriage and it is running away from you, until your face is like the goatskin in Africa. The harder you get, the more second-hand you become. You fix the hair from side to side and yet there is no marriage. Well, today you are going to get married in Jesus' name, because the God of impossibility is in the house.

Let me talk to the Nigerian witches who have got permanent stay in Great Britain, let me also talk to the Ghana witches who also got permanent stay. Britain is the worst place for you to get comfortable in, because Christianity is spreading in the cities.

Today, I have news that may not be good to witches but it is good news to the Christians here because you are serving the God of Elijah. There is a power that you can get, that when you speak, you will be able to kill the witches who are trying to bewitch you. When they come to your doorstep, you can use the power of God to kill them by the words of your own mouth.

The Ignorance of the Theologians

There are issues on which I disagree with the theologians of this generation. They do not know God because they do not understand the Bible. I can call them illiterate to the things of God. These theologians are uneducated and lack understanding. They study the Bible at college and get degrees but they are still illiterate. The Bible teaches us clearly, that if we do not put what the Bible says into practice then there is no need to learn about the Bible.

The Bible does not say that you are to study the words and just go and speak about what Apostle Paul, Moses, Elijah and the other persons mentioned in the Bible did. Can God only be the God of Elijah's days in the Old Testament? In the New Testament, which is our time, we read about radical men of God. Somebody say, "radical!" A radical person is not somebody you can joke with. He can kill you if you are not careful.

Do not hate me. I am teaching you how to destroy the witches. Suppose a witch comes here and destroys me, who will lose? The people who love me will lose, and also my mother will lose her son. Who will come and preach here? Listen here, the gospel we preach is not a joke and the salvation we receive is the same salvation Apostles Peter and John received. We can refer to the lives of great men in the Bible in the Old Testament who were before Jesus.

But let us talk about the Apostle called Peter

Apostle Peter was a radical man. When they tried to arrest Jesus he cut off a man's ears. He took his knife because he was a serious man. Jesus returned the ear in its rightful place. To the people who are spiritually mature, that was a miracle. This showed the power of the man they were persecuting. He healed the wounded man's ear instantly.

Jesus told Peter put away the knife in his pocket. That could mean "when I am not here, deal with them." He could have told Peter to get rid of the knife, but he did not. He could have rebuked Peter and told him that he had done wrong. Did Jesus rebuke Peter and told him that he had done wrong? Don't joke with Jesus, if you do wrong he will tell you! Apostle Peter was a preacher whose shadow healed the sick.

The Anointing destroys the Enemy

There is a man by the name of Apostle Paul who also did many miracles, signs and wonders in the New Testament. His jacket when taken to the sick brought healing instantly to the sick people. The handkerchief of Apostle Paul was also used as a point of contact to heal the sick. This man was formerly a bad man. He was a killer before Jesus met with him. He received great anointing when Jesus met him, and he was able to heal the sick and cast out demons in the name of Jesus.

Apostle Paul was a preacher who reached a level that he was able to minister to the governor, and he preached to people and told them about Christ. The people were happy to know that Jesus can save them. But there was someone who came along one day to distract the people from paying attention to the gospel of Jesus Christ. That person also wanted to pollute the mind of the people who were being ministered to by Apostle Paul. Folks, this is New Testament and it is still happening today. We are talking about witchcraft!

Most of our Christian brethren are praying for the witches, so that they can keep on bewitching them. The witches have made you single, they have blocked your womb so that you cannot give birth. The witches have destroyed your job. Some of you were working but a witch wanted your job and bewitched you so that you lose it. The next day you are sacked and you go to church and say "Allelujah, I love the Lord. Praise God, God will fight for me, I love my enemies."

Jesus said in the scripture to love your enemies, but he never said we were to love witches. Come on! People are misinterpreting things, but when I am finished with you, you are going to be dangerous. I am a dangerous man! You cannot bring to me witchcraft, and live to see tomorrow. The same power that is within me was in Elijah and

Moses. I walk by that power and if you challenge me, I will survive.

What you believe is what apply to you. Keep in your mind what I mentioned to you earlier, that it was not God's plan or God's decision to kill the fifty people who came to arrest Elijah. It was Elijah's decision to let God kill people, who came to kill him.

Now, Elijah had to make a decision. Either to love his enemies by allowing them to arrest him and take him for the King to kill or to save his own life by letting his enemies die. He had to decide to live so that he could continue to minister and to later on impart the anointing to Elisha, in a agreement with God's plan for his life.

If Elijah had been careless with his life, then there would not be any Elisha to do miracles. If the witches kill a minister, they terminate God's plan to pass the anointing from one generation to another. Now you need to know that you are more special in God's eyes, than witches, and homosexuals. Only your foolish behaviours and ignorance can let you die for nothing.

Faith comes by hearing and hearing the word of God. If you believe that when witches look at you they will die, then they will die because that is your faith. Somebody says, "good new!" Alleluia!

The radical power in the New Testament

Now let us continue with the ministry of Apostle Paul. It is obvious that this man did not care. Don't joke with Apostle Paul. Even though he found Peter with a ministry that was in existence from the time he was with Jesus, Paul rebuked him when he was wrong. Peter liked to pretend, he behaved one way with the Gentiles in the sight of the Jews and in a different way when the Jews were absent. Paul publicly rebuked him to be himself and stop pretending. Apostle Paul was very bold.

If Pastor Mensah has the same Holy Ghost that Apostle Paul had, he will make people like Elymas blind here, if they try to spoil God's plan. Jesus of Apostle Paul made Elmyas blind.

The Bible says in **Acts 13:4-12** *"Having been sent by the Holy Spirit, Barnabas and Saul went to Seleucia and sailed from there to the island of Cyprus. When they arrived at Salamis, they preached the word of God in the synagogues."* They had John Mark with them to help in the work.

They went all the way across the island to Paphos, where they met a certain magician named Bar-Jesus, a Jew who claimed to be a prophet. He was a friend of the governor of the island, Sergius Paulus, who was an intelligent man. The governor called Barnabas and Saul (Apostle Paul) before him because he wanted to hear the word of God. But they were opposed by the magician Elymas (that is his name in Greek), who tried to turn the governor away from the faith. Then Saul - also known as Paul - was filled with the Holy Spirit; he looked straight at the magician and said; "You son of the Devil! You are the enemy of everything that is good.

You are full of all kinds of evil tricks, and you always keep trying to turn the Lord's truths into lies! The Lord's hand will come down on you now; you will be blind and will not see the light of day for a time.'

At once Elymas felt a dark mist cover his eyes and he walked around trying to find someone lead him by the hand. When the governor as what had happened, he believed; for he was greatly amazed at the teaching about the Lord." I am a radical teacher. I can teach with boldness because I do not fear anything. What I am teaching you ladies and gentlemen, I know it will enable you to exist in this wicked generation.

When Apostle Paul looked at Elymas it was not a look of peace. It was not a "look" for healing of the sick neither was it a "look" to make someone comfortable. It was a dangerous "look", because Apostle Paul had the intention of harming the magician. The magician got a look that rebuked him. The magician who was a human being was physically harmed for doing wrong, when he tried to spoil the work of God. I am not adding or changing anything, what I am writing about is the word of God. What God is able to do, the believers of today cannot understand that He can do it!

Some people have dangerous neighbours who are bewitching them and their children. They left their homeland to come to Britain for a better life and after thirty years, they realize that things are not any better. These people are struggling with the bills for daily living. Their children are having problems with drugs and have become rebellious. When they discover that their lives are getting worse, they begin to attend church to see what God will do. God is not going to do anything until you make a decision, about what you want Him to do. God will never do anything until you tell Him, what you want Him to do!

It is not because you want to live this way, but you are so ignorant and foolish in believing that you are being loving and generous when you pray for the witches to live and be blessed. Apostle Paul called Elymas, "son of the Devil." Now, did the devil gave birth to a human being? Why did Paul call this man the son of the Devil? Elymas did evil tricks to confuse people and he tried to turn the truth of God's holy words into lies.

The Bible says we are the children of God, through Jesus Christ. Therefore whosoever that is against us or opposes the gospel of Jesus Christ is the son of the devil.

Many of you believe that you are being humble when you love the witches who are your enemies. That is what you have in your mind. Now, let me tell you this once more, Paul was never humble to witches. He dealt with them, with God's POWER.

When Moses spoke, he spoke with POWER, when Elijah spoke, he spoke with POWER. Everything that God says or does, it is with POWER. Our Kingdom, where Jesus Christ reigns, is a heavenly Kingdom, with great power. It has all the weapons to protect God's people from any destruction that satan wants to bring to them here on earth.

Lack of knowledge and confusion of Christians today

God did not create Adam to suffer here on earth. He made Adam to enjoy his life. It is the devil, whose power is witchcraft - that caused God's people to be deceived and become cursed in the beginning. It is Lucifer who appeared to Eve and succeeded in polluting her mind so that he could cause confusion and destruction. Witches are using the power of Lucifer to do the same thing right now.

Come on, listen to me if a witch is able to bewitch you whilst you are a Christian attending church; then that would mean that Lucifer is more powerful than Jesus. Well, let me tell you now that Jesus Christ is more powerful and He is the Lord. The witches' source of power is useless in the presence of Jesus.

If you are attending church and a witch can make you to lose your job, what are you doing in the church? If a witch can make you single and destroy your education, what are you doing in the church? That means that the devil is greater than the God you serve. I believe that you understand what I am talking about. Many Christians - "godly" people, are suffering and dying right now under witchcraft because they believe that they should be nice and kind to the witches. Some do not want anymore to know about their problems and so they say they are "all right".

The country is full of witchcraft, but I believe that the witches in England should only be able to bewitch homosexuals and other ungodly people. They should not be able to bewitch those who are "born again" and speaking in tongues. If someone says they are "filled with the Holy Spirit" and a witch is later able to bewitch them and control them like a remote control; then that is a "dead holy spirit" not the Holy Spirit of Almighty God.

What kind of Holy Spirit do you have? Is it a small, or a weak, or a baby Holy Spirit that you have? Is it a temporary Holy Ghost that filled you?. I want to wake you up, for too long Christians have been sleeping. Put down that "dead holy spirit" and I will introduce you to one that will make the witches blind, the same Holy Spirit that Apostle Paul had.

You may not like me because I never went to any school to study Theology. I do not care what you think, as I have already decided that I will use the Bible the way it is. I am not a foolish person. I am able to read something and to do exactly what it is telling me to do. If the Bible says to me this is what Apostle Paul did, then that is what I am going to do. I will not wait for someone to come from the University to tell me what I am supposed to do.

Magicians are dangerous to weak Christians

It was the Holy Spirit that had sent Paul and Barnabas to Seleucia which is in Europe, and I thank God that Elymas was made blind so that he would not stop the work.

Who is a magician? Someone who is skilled in magic is called a magician. That is a dangerous person - a wicked person, and he can do great harm to people. They get their power from the devil to do magic. They try to do things to persuade people that they have the power of Almighty God. Like Pharaoh's magicians, who tried to copy the things Moses had done by God's power. This man Bar-Jesus, called Elymas was a magician who claimed to be a prophet, and even today there are many so called "prophets" who are using magical powers.

They prophesy to people through their magical power and they claim that they are godly people. They use the name of God the Father, the Son and the Holy Spirit. They prophesy things that do not come to pass.
Some are called fortune-tellers. They try to tell you your future and sometimes put fear in you about what is supposed to happen.

False Prophets

I prophesied to Pastor Mensah years ago, when they came to us from Holland. He and his wife were trying to get a baby. I told him that within one year, God was going to give them a baby boy. They never got a baby girl, they got a son, who you are now seeing here.

There are some prophets who will tell you that you are going to get married, but because they are false prophets you still remain single. They are like Elymas, magicians who will confuse your minds. You can believe that you are in a church listening to God and seeing his power, only to discover that the Pastor is a "false prophet", who is using magical powers.

You need to see the "fruits" that come from a person's ministry before you submit to them. If you do not see me wearing shoes, do not come to me for prayers to get shoes. If I am not married, do not come to me for prayers to get married. You will remain single. If I am poor, do not come to me for prayers to get wealth, because you will never get it. I can only give you something I already have.

It is very important to find out

about any man of God who claims that he is anointed. If someone is a drunkard, they cannot successfully lay hands on anyone in prayers to be "filled with the Holy Spirit". It will not happen. The person they pray for can only become a drunkard like them.

I am a radical teacher, which is why I am able to write a dangerous prayer book. I have the same faith of Elijah and Elisha. The Bible says that Elymas "was a friend of the governor of the island, Sergius Paulus, who was an intelligent man." The governor, although he was an intelligent man, he did not know that Elymas was using a power that he got from the devil to influence him.

Folks, you can be intelligent and having PhD. Degrees, but that does not prevent you from being fooled by magicians and to become messed up.

The Bible says in **Hosea 4:6** that *"God's people perish because of lack* *of knowledge."* This is true! If you have ears, hear what the Bible says.

The Testimony that destroys the works of the devil

Dear child of God, Greetings to you in the most precious and matchless name of our soon coming Lord and saviour Jesus Christ. We are indeed glad and rejoice in the Lord in presenting to you the life transforming testimony of Evangelist Patrick Deya. We trust and hope that you will be blessed as we take you to the life of Evangelist Patrick Deya.

"...The stone which the builders rejected, the same is become the head of the corner: this is the Lord's doing, and it is marvelous in our eyes." -
Mt. 21:42.

Evangelist Patrick Deya was born in the year 1960. He was brought up in a family that did not know the supernatural existence of the Almighty God. In the course of time, his mother received Salvation and was able to guide him. However, at that time he was only attending routine church services and not really acquainted with the Word of God.

Sometime in the year 1971, Patrick who had been taking the calves to the river to let them drink water, had to cross a junction road; within a fraction of a second, he had started to tremble and to feel excessively cold.

This was very frightening, as the weather that day was moderately warm, yet he was experiencing a sudden cold. Patrick made his way home, covered himself, in a thick blanket, and rested in the pasture that was just outside his house. His mother Monica Nono Deya, on her way to fetch water from the river, saw someone resting in the pasture with a blanket on a bright and warm day. She hurried over to investigate and to her amazement discovered that it was her son Patrick.

Patrick was unable to stand, as he could not move any of his limbs. He had to be carried inside the house by his mother, to the bedroom. Gradually his joints, shoulders and knees became inflicted with pain.

The next morning his father contacted a witchdoctor by the name of Obo Nyo Guunde. The witchdoctor visited Patrick every morning and evening. He tried all his medicines; which was purely extracted from witch-hazel (medicinal leaves), to see if any of them could make Patrick well. Sadly, the only result was that Patrick's knees, shoulders and thighs began to swell. Incapable of bending his joints, he set himself moving on his knees, he became a cripple. Whenever there was heavy rainfall in the night, Patrick would not sleep but would weep until the rain stopped.

Patrick experienced a sudden occurrence, of an unknown disease. His older sister Joyce Aluoch Oyanda requested her mother to take Patrick to the Nandi Hill Hospital, to get medical attention. At the hospital, German white doctors began to treat Patrick, trying to counteract his disease. The doctors were incapable of tracing the disease even through X-rays. His thighs had begun to swell in an unusual way; this forced the surgeon to cut open the affected area about eight inches, in his effort to detect the disease. This surgery proved futile. An armchair was now his only place to rest.

It so happened that a man of God by the name of Peter Okello Jullu from South Nyanza, dressed in a long white robe, came to Patricks village home. He proclaimed to all, that God had sent him to the village. He was a stranger to the village folks.

The man of God visited the Deya's home and without knowing anything about the family beforehand, revealed that he had seen in a vision a young boy whose hands and legs were no longer functioning and also an old man who was a drunkard. He inquired of Monica Deya, the identity of the two persons, and was told that it was her youngest son Patrick and her husband. She then informed him, her son Patrick was hospitalized but she could take him from the hospital with a written permission.

Patrick was brought home. The man of God had been praying for him, from 9 o'clock in the night until 3 am, when suddenly the boy collapsed and fell to the floor in an unconscious state. Patrick's parents thought Peter Okello

Jullu was sure to kill their son. They did not let the man of God to know what was in their minds. This thought gave them great pain and agony and they quietly began to weep. The man of God told them to cry for God, and not weep for their son.

The man of God prayed for the boy on a day-to-day basis, at regular intervals - 6 am; 10 am; 12 noon; 3 p.m.; and 6 p.m. On the eve of the Sabbath day he would direct the entire family to finish with the house duties, so that they could fast in total prayers the next day.

The prayers were answered; the swollen infected area on the shoulders, knees and thighs burst open, resulting in excessive discharge of yellowish matter. In line with the discharge of pus, unusual minutes bones - 15 in number - came out of his right shoulder.

"Surely there is no enchantment

against Jacob, neither is there any division against Israel: according to this time it shall be said of Jacob and of Israel, what hath God wrought!" - **Numbers 23:23.** Hallelujah!

Patrick was instructed by the man of God to walk; a walking stick was used so that he could stand on his feet. The preacher constantly knelt down in the presence of the Lord for a breakthrough in the life of Patrick. Great is our Lord and He is greatly to be praised. Hallelujah! Patrick began to walk independently - he no longer required any support. The servant of God, Peter Okello Jullu, prophesied over Patrick and his brother Gilbert Deya. He told them that they would work only for the Kingdom of God, taking the eternal message of hope to the nations of the world.

"...And as ye go, preach, saying, The Kingdom of Heaven is at hand. Heal the sick, cleanse the lepers, raise

the dead, cast out devils: freely ye have received, freely give." **Mt. 10:7-8.** Praise the Lord!

In the year 1973, Patrick was admitted to the school for standard one. His father who was a drunkard, would leave the home in the morning and return late at night, staying away all day without caring how his family survived. His older brother, Gilbert Deya, who toiled hard as a stonecutter and later on as a toilet cleaner, provided the money for Patrick's education. In spite of the fact that he was able to walk, there was a discharge of yellowish matter. Due to the intensive flow of pus from his shoulders and knees, a visible appearance of cavity was formed on the sides of his arms and knees. Patrick constantly had to use his handkerchief for wiping off the yellowish matter from the side of his arms and knees; the wounds would also give out an unpleasant odour, hence the teacher decided to put him by the sides of the wall.

Patrick did very well in all his academics. In the year 1975, he was completely healed and made whole by the power of God. Praise God!.

"I will put none of these diseases upon thee, which I have brought upon the Egyptians: for I am the Lord that healeth thee." **Ex. 15:26** Hallelujah!

Patrick and his mother went to the place where Peter Okello Jullu was holding his crusade. The crusade was divided into two sessions. There was a short waiting period between the two sessions, and during that time, Patrick and some of the boys moved along the river to bathe.

As he went into the river to bathe, he found that he was being carried away by a vigorous whirlpool (circular flow of currents) and was sure to be affected. Patrick was about to drown when he saw a bright streak of light coming from heaven towards him. A song was set down in words on the rays of light, which read as follows:

"Kuomi Kuomi Nachiwoni To Inimia An'go, Koro Akeloni ee, Gweth Moa Epolo" This means, "For you, for you, I am giving to you. What are you going to give me? Now I am bringing to you the blessings from heaven."

Patrick had not come across this song before, yet he began to sing it, making melody in his heart. Before he could conclude the song, the boys had managed to take him out of the river.

Meanwhile, in the crusade, a woman of God was prophesying that somebody was relating to a moment of death, and she requested the congregation to pray for the dying soul. Monica Deya, who was present in the crusade, was unaware of the near death of her son, Patrick. The boys entered the crusade and Patrick testified of being rescued by Jesus Christ, the

Almighty God. He heard the same song that was set down in words on the rays of light coming from heaven, being sung by the people in the crusade and for the first time he began to sing. There was a great anointing in the crusade. Glory be to the name of our Lord Jesus Christ!

Although he was healed by the power of God, Patrick had not experienced Salvation.

In the month of June, 1978, Patrick began to suffer from insanity. Whilst seated in his classroom he suddenly began to weep with a loud noise, and he also lost his memory. Patrick took off his uniform and naked the galloped away uncontrollably. In his imagination he had seen many people chasing him ferociously to destroy him with spears. The teachers, parents and the entire school tried to take hold of him. He was girded with ropes, because he would strike people repeatedly. He would speak not to men, but to the demons that were afflicting him. Patrick was demonized, being controlled by 12 spirits, the chief of which was Odera (Great grandfather of Patrick).

Odera was a sorcerer who lived in bushes. He was skilled in magic and witchcraft invoking supernatural powers to influence events. Odera had died in the bushes even before Patrick's mother could get married. Patrick's mother took him to a church called Luong Mogik Koduma Yimbo, where people, who are in requisite need of prayers, would come and stay until their needs are met. Mary Otieno (sister of Patrick), accompanied her mother and Patrick. Prayers were being offered at 6 am; 12 am; 3 pm; and 6 pm. The rope was taken off Patrick and he was brought to a man, who was to flog him with a cane. The belief was that, the demons would be driven out from his life by caning. As the man began to cane Patrick, he ran several kilometers afar off and hid in the interior bushes.

Unable to find her absconded son, Monica Deya decided to go back to her home in the village. Patrick who was hiding in the bushes saw a man on a motorcycle; it was his brother Gilbert Deya. Gilbert had travelled all the way from Nairobi for about six hours, in order to see his brother alone. The sound of the motorcycle was pleasing to Patrick's ears. Gilbert saw his brother hiding in the bushes, and called him. He carried him back to the village home and told his Mother that he wanted to take Patrick to his home in Nairobi.

Patrick had an attack one night that was remarkable. A large number of people gathered to help, they wanted to take him to the hospital but he refused to get into the car. He resisted them, and as he was very strong no one could put him in the car. The problem was such that the civil force, which maintains public order, was called. The police took out their guns in order to threaten him, and gradually his aggressiveness was under control. They then took him to the Mathare Mental Hospital in Nairobi. Monica Deya visited him in the hospital, she did not see any sign of changes in his behaviour.

The evil spirits controlling Patrick had made him to get underneath the cars and huge vehicles, in the city of Nairobi. Fearing that she may lose her son in this city, Patrick's mother decided to take him back to her village.

Patrick was unclean, naked, hiding in the bushes eating rot and exchanging ideas with nonsense and worthless things. He would direct his eyes at the papers around him and utter words to them, making sounds distinctly expressing amusement. Indoors he would ruin the materials objects (furniture etc.) in the house. He strongly disliked light and was delighted to remain in darkness. As Patrick would beat the people around him, he was bound with chains. However, the spirits dominating him would untie the chains.

The demonic spirits which were possessing Patrick, used him as an instrument (medium) to speak out that someone in the family was sure to die, even before the dawn of the first day of August. This was a song he frequently sang. Monica Deya did not consider that this could be a prediction, she thought that he was uttering words due to insanity.

On the first day of August, 1978, there was a sudden death in the family. It was Wilson Ojwang, the brother of Patrick, who being a victim of witchcraft lost his life in a major road accident. The prediction of evil was fulfilled. Unexpectedly, Achieng Ochuodho, a driver of a bus from Missori to Kisumu also died.

Monica Deya attended the funeral ceremony. There were three types of collective units formed:- one was for social gathering for the purpose of dancing, the second was for those drinking liquor and making merry and the third consisted of the people listening to the Word of God.

Monica Deya sat in the third unit, among the women. The Word of God being shared by the preacher was appropriate to her life and her family. The other woman who were supposed to be listening were speaking among themselves in soft hushed tones. Monica Deya changed her seat, she went closer to the preacher. She wanted to listen attentively, to the voice of God. The preacher, Harson Odoyo Odhiambo from South Nyanza Awendo quoted, *"I know thy works and where thou dwellest, even where Satan's seat is: and thou holdest fast my name, and hast not denied my faith..."* **Rev. 2:13.**

Monica Deya strongly believed that this verse of Scripture was indeed pertaining to her life and family. She was an anointed woman of God, a spirit filled woman who was also a deacon in her church.. It was at this appointed hour, that she realized there were signs of demonic forces operating in her home, and that satan was dwelling and inhabiting the seat in her house (husband being an alcoholic, son being an insane man and her daughter being affected by epileptics).

"Who shall separate us from the love of Christ? Shall tribulation or distress, or persecution, or famine, or nakedness, or peril, or sword?" - **Romans 8:35.**

Monica Deya had greatly desired to invite this preacher to her home, and she got her heart's desire when her friend by the name of Ambiche, brought the man of God to her house.

The servant of God, entered the village home of Monica Deya. She told him that Patrick would beat him, if he saw him. However, he replied that Patrick could not put his hand on him, because he had the power of God Almighty in him. The man of God requested a place to stay, where he could fast and pray for three days and three nights, in order to uproot the demonic activities that were present in the house.

Monica Deya cleared her kitchen, in order to make room for the preacher. The man of God began to pray to destroy the works of the enemy. Later he requested that Patrick be brought to him for prayers. His parents searched for him in the village and in the bushes, but they could not find him. His mother had a "word of knowledge" to open the doors of Wilson's room that was kept locked for several years. Praise the Lord! She found Patrick in the room.

Apparently, while the preacher was seated in the house, he had entered the door along the passage without noticing him. Patrick sat in the dark corner of the room conversing with the "worthless things" until his mother offered him tea. He finished the tea, and became aware of the stranger in the room. He rushed over to the man of God as if to beat him, but found that he could not reach out his hand and instead fell to the ground.

The preacher, Harson Odoyo Odhiambo pronounced the words of faith, and with authority cast out the demons, which had been tormenting Patrick for two years. Every kind of familiar spirit was cast out one by one. The man of God later requested clothes to be brought for Patrick, who was now in his sober mind. What a mighty God we serve! *"And they come to Jesus, and see him that was possessed with the devil, and had the legion, sitting, and clothed, and in his right hand mind: and they were afraid.."* **Mark 5:15**

Hallelujah!

Now, there was a tremendous transformation in the life of Patrick. Praise the Lord! He was well balanced; well mannered, well spoken and no more was he an insane boy. The preacher taught him about Salvation. He accepted Jesus Christ as his Lord and Saviour and was advised that he also needed the anointing of the Holy Spirit, as Salvation without the Holy Spirit is dead. Right away he experienced the anointing of the Holy Ghost.

Patrick consequently engaged in the ministry carried out by the servant of God. The anointing that was on the life of Harson Odoyo Odhiambo was now being transferred to him. Praise God!

In the year 1980, his brother Gilbert Deya had him enrolled in a technical school for tailoring, and he was also trained to drive; thereby

Patrick set up his own business for his livelihood. Praise the Lord!

Today, Patrick is no longer Patrick, but Evangelist Patrick Deya and he is now the father of four children. The prophetic word that God had spoken through His son, Peter Okello Jullu is fulfilled, Hallelujah!

God Almighty enabled Evangelist Patrick Deya and his brother Archbishop Gilbert Deya to carry this message of hope to the nations of the world with power, authority, divine healing, prophetic gifts and word of knowledge - to all people of different faiths. Through Gilbert Deya Ministries, thousands of people have experienced the resurrection power of Jesus Christ, and have come to salvation. Their vision and mission is to carry the oracles of God confirmed by mighty signs and wonders to the perishing millions around the globe. All glory and honour belongs to our Lord Jesus Christ alone! Amen.

Healing of Cancer

My name is penninah Waithera. I am suffering from cancer of the uterus, which cause terrible pain. I am bleeding blood mixed with water. Over the years, I have watched my family live in agony as my mother Rebecca brought much confusion to my dad and in the lives of her children. On many occasion she invited witch doctors to our home. They did many strange rituals on us, cutting us with blades. She was always accusing my Dad of going out with other woman. There was always great confusion in our family, and curses that caused death, mental sickness, bad luck and singleness to affect us.

We are eleven children by both parents. My brother Jorum died by car accident - the car ran on him when he was riding a bicycle. It was painful to lose our brother in such a sudden and tragic circumstance. Five months later, my brother Joseph was accused by his wife of having other women, just like what my mum did to my dad. His wife went to the witch doctor to seek a solution to this problem - he later died of asthma. My brother Joshua Kibugi became an alcoholic and developed a coughing sickness. He coughed blood for a while, until he died. It is said that he died from T.B. One month later, his lovely daughter Mukina also died.

My elder brother James is mentally sick, he can't figure out anything. My brother Jonah is having a swollen leg, epilepsy and he is also suffering from mental problems. My brother Jeremiah stopped eating for no apparent reason, and he also became mentally ill. He was admitted at the Mathare Mental Hospital in Nairobi, Kenya. To our surprise, frogs began to appear in every room he stayed in. Frogs would mysteriously appear in his room even when we moved to the city, his room was always full of frogs.

My brother Joel is also an alcoholic. He is always imagining people chasing to kill him - to me that means he too is mentally sick. My youngest brother John has been married twice. His first wife divorced him and left him with 3 children. He is now living a life of war with second wife. The woman is fighting in witchcraft.

It is sad, that my father, my mother and eleven of us - a family of fourteen (14) are living without happiness. I never understood what was happening, until now. I became aware that the problems that were affecting us were caused by witchcraft. I learned this, when I started attending teaching services held at the Gilbert Deya Ministries. Our family has been suffering because of generation curses. I got married to a white English man, who was working in Kenya and had a very good job as a teacher.

My husband got involved and was having affairs with the student girls. One of the girls confronted me face to face. She told me that I could not do anything to stop her because she loved my husband. I also followed my mother's foot-steps, of moving from witchdoctor to witchdoctor, astrologer to astrologer, palm reader to palm reader to get help in my marriage.

I tried everything I knew, to protect my marriage. In the end, my husband died a mysterious death. I will never be able to explain how it happened. He was a good caring husband. He bought lands for me and built houses. Nobody can tell whether the witches I attended to protect my marriage bewitched him, or whether it was caused by the jealousy of people towards me being married to a white man or whether it was a natural death. I became confused after his death, as I had lost a very good breadwinner.

After he died, my wicked mother who introduced the entire family to witchcraft raised war against me. She confronted me and demanded that I should share the properties my husband left for me with my mentally sick brothers. As I refused to do so, she cursed me. She swore that nothing I do will succeed. She said I will never get married and that I will die in agony and my children will see nothing. Praise God, I received the opportunity to fly to London to seek help from Jesus at the Gilbert Deya Ministries. I used to watch their programmes on TV, whilst I was in Kenya.

I thank God for the privilege to be in London. I believe that God will heal me and deliver me from generation curses. At the moment I am suffering and in great pain because of cancer. I am bleeding blood mixed with water. My prayer is that the God of Archbishop Deya will deliver me from this affliction and also set my family free.

Testimony: Sis. Yvonne

In 1989, there were a series of incidents and events in my life, which overwhelmed me and I became a very confused woman. I had problems to concentrate on my subject, and I begun to hear "voices" sometimes arguing in my head, or telling me what to do or say. I also suffered from a personality disorder. My daily routine was upset, and became very difficult as I had mood swings and was at times very disruptive. I was recommended to see Dr. Frank Knight, a senior psychiatrist at the University Hospital of the West Indies - Ward 21. I was admitted there for some time, and later became an out-patient. Nevertheless my situation remained the same. I decided to keep my condition a secret from my family, although they could see what was happening in my life.

My mother never believed in or practiced witchcraft. She was brought up in the Church of God and she was very strict on church attendance, and regular study of the Bible. My family could not understand what was happening to me and I knew that they were worried and embarrassed. I tried to explain to them, that I was being tormented by the rulers of darkness from the kingdom of satan.

This mental suffering was inherited from past generations and was being enforced by demonic spirits, although I had been brought up in the Church of God of Jamaica and was a Christian from childhood. The power of witchcraft over my life and the resulting breakdown of my marriage caused me to temporarily lose my mind. I sought help in Jamaica from various "faith" healers through "so called" friends, whom I later found out were really my enemies. One of the most famous "faith healer" of the Caribbean, a man known as "Kapo" from Water House, Kingston, Jamaica (now deceased) tried to heal me by the power of divination. Secretly, I also sought the help of other mediums and occult practitioners (who are also now dead) but my situation only changed for the worse, as the demon harassed me even more. I began to burn my clothes and any household items in public view. I wrote on the walls of the house as the "voice" would instruct me to do all manner of crazy things. I would sometimes hear a knock at my door and when I opened it no one could be seen by me, but I would sense a presence.

There were times when it was not an easy task to keep me in control and I would get angry very easily. I was on medication, but I stopped myself from taking the drugs that was administered by the clinic to keep me calm because it made me to operate like a "zombie." I had a dream one night of Jesus coming to visit me.

Jesus sent a messenger to call me. The messenger told me I did not need to take any more medication; I was to come to see Jesus without taking them. I agreed and started running towards Jesus. I saw a bright light and a flowing white garment and where his face was meant to be I saw a cross. Suddenly, I felt as if I was caught up in the air then Jesus held me in his arms and started dancing with me. I woke up that morning and flushed all the tablets in the toilet. Even after this dream, for six years I suffered mental anguish and my life was at times like a roller coaster. I lost weight and it was obvious to people around me that something was wrong with me, as I was too ill to care how I looked.

I am now aware that, I was kept

from suicide and serious harm and danger by Jesus Christ, who is my Lord and Saviour. The only thing that kept me was the love of Jesus, and His faithfulness and mercy towards me. Praise God!

I joined the Gilbert Deya Ministries in London in 1995. Archbishop Deya had just started the Ministry and he was trying to find a place for his meetings when I met him. I was homeless at that time, as I had been evicted from where I was living and in one year had lived in over 14 different homes in various areas of London.

Meeting Archbishop Deya was a divine appointment because I was attending Deeper Life Bible Church and yet my situation was grim. I was contemplating suicide because I had given up hope and in my heart I was angry with God for allowing me to suffer so badly. The Archbishop gave

Authority over Satan

me a prophetic word within minutes of meeting me. He said God told him that there would be "great anointing" on my life and that God would raise me up like Apostle Paul.

Archbishop Deya told me that I was "wornderful" and "good." He saw me through the eyes of Jesus and knew that God had not rejected me. He took me everywhere with him, driving around London. We went to Croydon to view a building, as Archbishop was seeking a place for his meetings. On the day, I saw a little boy who was knocked down by a motor vehicle - receive his healing in the name of Jesus. The Lord used the Archbishop to hold the crushed and bleeding body to his chest and to pray the prayer of faith. Life returned to the little boy and his broken bones were restored instantly. This miracle convinced me that Archbishop Gilbert Deya was a man greatly anointed by God. His prayers were sincere and I felt the awesome presence of God in his meetings.

As a true man of God, the Archbishop took an interest in my welfare and placed me in the care of female ministers from his Ministry; namely Sis. Jean Casey and Sis. Wendy Crosbie. I was not healed overnight, it was a process but my faith in God was restored as I held on to the prophetic words given to me by Archbishop Deya. Once again I began to study the word of God daily. The word of God became my life, my only option for survival.

The demons were cast out of my body, but my "flesh" had to be disciplined. I attended the meetings every day for many months. My mind was restored and renewed by the "finger of God" and Archbishop trained me to work with his deliverance team. Within one year, I could clearly remember all the scriptures I had learnt as a child.

Whereas before I was hearing voices from demons, now the Holy Spirit speaks clearly to my mind. The Holy Spirit rebukes me, counsels me and reassures me that I am loved. This is amazing to many persons who have shared with me that they found it difficult to listen, and to hear from God even when they read the scriptures with much fasting and prayers.

After deliverance, I felt compelled to preach and would do so at every opportunity, even on the streets in London. I would loudly praise the Lord and was on "fire" for God. In every service I would give the signal whenever there was a manifest presence of God and it was a joke to many people as I praised and worshipped and danced to the Lord with abandon.

Archbishop Deya warned me that I would be kicked out of "dead" and "compromising" churches with this kind of anointing which God had released in his ministry. He told me that I was to expect great persecutions and trials. I did not believe this at the time, and so I was quite unprepared when his words began to prove true.

I began to preach in other churches and later enrolled as a student at the International Bible Institute of London (I.B.I.O.L.). I did the one (1) year Diploma in Christian Ministries course and during that time became a member of London City Church. Archbishop warned me what could happen with the mixture of different doctrines. He also told me that I did not need to attend any Bible College because the Holy Ghost had me in his classroom already and had anointed me. Nevertheless, I chose to an extended period of over three years. I returned to Jamaica and also visited other countries overseas.

As I visited other Churches, life

proved different from what I had expected. I discovered that there were Pastors who did not believe in demonstrating the power of God, as it was done in the time of Apostle Paul and Peter in the Bible. I was casting out demons in the name of Jesus and I would often see demonic spirits manifesting in Ministers, even as they preached from their pulpits. I would from time to time receive "Word of knowledge" as to their true spiritual condition and I was able to discern the fruit in their lives. This caused me to receive strong opposition from some persons who were living double lives. I was preached about, lied on, rejected and betrayed by fellow brothers and sisters in Christ.

Whenever I shared my testimony, giving God the glory and praise for what he had done in my life many were offended. They could not understand why God chose to favour me, because to them I was unworthy. Some, who had accepted me before they heard my testimony, would begin to shun me and treat me as if I am a second-class citizen because of my past. I believe this is because they do not know or understand the Word of God, which clearly states that if anyone is in Christ they have become a new creature and that the old life and behaviour has passed away. My dear readers, even some dear Church Leaders-persons who call themselves Pastors, after hearing my detailed testimony they no longer wanted anything to do with me and would begin to judge me by past and to treat me with disdain.

Can you image that there are Christians who doubt that Jesus is able to completely heal a mind that is "unsound" and to bring victory to a life that had been tormented and made useless by the power of the devil?

Yet, the very same person claim

that they are 'anointed'. Can someone rightly claim to be 'anointed' if they do not believe. God's power to be trustworthy - to permanently heal?

Mark 5:15 *"And when they came to Jesus, they saw the man who used to have the mob of demons in him. He was sitting there, clothed and in his right mind; and they were all afraid."*

My prayers is that these "church goers" will receive deliverance from their ignorance of God's ability and power to change a life, and that the spirit of unbelief and doubt will be cast out of their lives forever in Jesus' name. I also pray that anyone who is offended or ashamed because of this Testimony; will come to know Jesus, and get the revelation of Jesus Christ and His finished work at the cross.

It is sad to share that I was also spiritually abused; by beloved mentors who tried to manipulate me and also to control me in a negative way. I became deeply hurt and was like a wounded soldier as I was opposed and alienated by people whom I dear-publicly called - "Judas" by a beloved Pastor who had sought to control my life in a negative manner. This made me to become discouraged and for a time I lost my zeal for the Lord.

I started to become ill again as I began to compromise, seeking the acceptance and approval of humans because of fear of rejection.

But like the prodigal son I decided to returned to my father. I said I would not preach again, but I have repented and God has forgiven me. Praise God for his grace and mercy towards me. Unlike some leaders, Archbishop greeted me with the love of Christ and being a good shepherd he is still concerned that I fulfill my destiny as God planned it.

I praise God for Archbishop Deya, because I now realize that many of the persons who speak badly against him, do so out of jealousy and spite; yet this does not stop him from ministering to God's people in answer to the great commission he has received from Heaven.

I will be who God wants me to be and I will remain in the Gilbert Deya Ministries, until God moves me. One day soon, by God's grace I will give the full story of my life, this is an edited version. I am healed, my mind is restored and renewed and free from oppression. Jesus Christ is faithful! To God I give the glory, honour and praise! Amen.

Afterword
by Pastor Amos Deya

God has given me favour through the grace of His Son of Jesus Christ through the Ministry of dealing with the devil, casting them out, destroying them and rendering them powerless by the blood of Jesus.

The book I am presenting to you, is a tool of life changing author by Zola Quinnen, who went through hell by the power of witchcraft.

She missed the grave which swallowed her enemies. I am convinced Whoever shall read this book, shall overcome witches' power and their Wickedness.

May the Glory and the Annointing of the Holy Spirit flow to whosover reading this book in Jesus name.

355

Books
audio and visual Tapes
By Archbishop Deya

HOW TO RECEIVE PROSPERITY MIRACULOUSLY

In this book Archbishop Gilbert Deya combines biblical principles, with personal experiences for a powerful teaching on how to receive prosperity miraculously. There are also personal testimonies of members of his Ministry who are blessed because of his teachings.

By applying the principles outlined in this book, you will learn:

How to trust God in times of lack and claim the abundant life
How to overcome the curse of poverty
How to tithe your way out of debts and prevent satan from touching your finances
Plus much more!

We can be successful people in this world. (Psalms 34:10) We will not lack in Jesus' name, we must have more than enough!!!

This book explains how people suffer unknowingly as they pay the price of sins committed by their ancestors. These sins have brought stronghold of singleness, bareness, bad luck and having incurable diseases that terminate their lives.

Gilbert Deya explains clearly the origins of these problems of generational curses and the solution of these curses through the blood of Jesus.

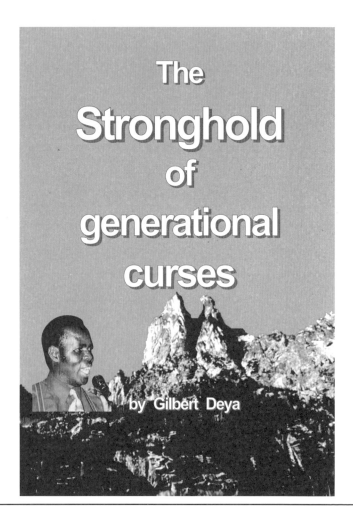

The Stronghold of generational curses

by Gilbert Deya

DEMONS CONFESS THEY KNOW JESUS

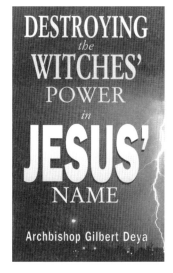

Here is a message from the Book of **Acts 19:13-20,** "Then certain of the vagabond Jews, exorcists, took upon them to call over them which had evil spirits in the name of the Lord Jesus, saying, we adjure you by Jesus whom Paul preacheth. And there were seven sons of one Sceva, a Jew, and chief of the priests, which did so. And the evil spirit answered and said, Jesus I know, and Paul I know, but who are ye? And the man in whom the evil spirit was, leaped on them, and overcame them and prevailed against them (beat them up) so that they fled out of that house, naked and wounded. And this was known to all the Jews and Greeks also dwelling at Ephesus and fear fell on them all, and the name of the Lord Jesus was magnified. And many that believeth came, and confessed and showed their deeds. Many of them also which used curious arts brought their books together and burned them before all men and counted the price of them, and found it fifty thousand pieces of silver. So mightily grew the word of God and pre-vailed."

Evil spirits can stay inside people. They are called unclean spirits or demons or spirits of the devil. Jesus knew very well that unclean spirits were in peoples lives. His ministry was a ministry that did not compromise with the devil. He came to destroy the work of Satan. That means, to cast devils out of people. Jesus gave his disciples power to cast out demons, that means to move them out in the name of Jesus.

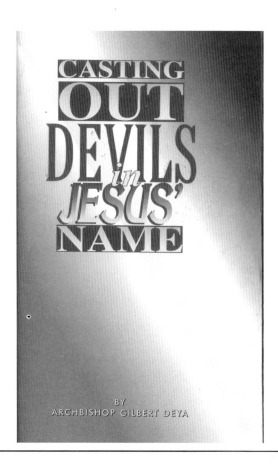

The world today has a lot spoken about sex. The advertisers many times try to sell their products portraying them as sexy. In this book Archbishop Gilbert Deya reveals the curses that are caused by the sexual behaviours that has resulted in our present day. He analysis a case where by a man had a sexual relationship with his wife and his mother in law sometimes in the same day and finally the man left his wife to live with his mother inlaw.

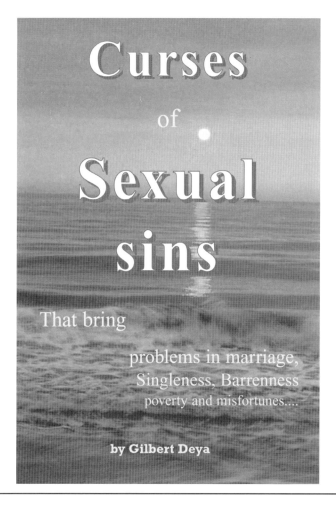

Curses

of

Sexual

sins

That bring

problems in marriage,
Singleness, Barrenness
poverty and misfortunes....

by Gilbert Deya

In this book

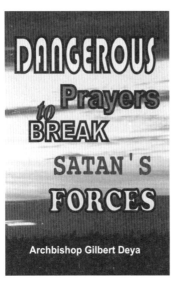

Archbishop Gilbert Deya

Psalms 35: 1 - 28

Oppose those who oppose me, LORD, and fight those who fight against me! Take your shield and armour and come to my rescue.

Lift up your spear and war axe against those who pursue me. Promise that you will save me. May those who try to kill me be defeated and disgraced! May those who plot against me be turned back and be confused!May they be like straw blown by the windas the angel of the LORD pursues them! May their path be dark and slippery while the angel of the LORD Strikes them down! Without any reason they laid a trap for me and dug a deep hole to catch me.

But destruction will catch them before they know it; they will be caught in their own trap and fall to their destruction!

Then I will be glad because of the LORD; I will be happy because he saved me. With all my heart I will say to the LORD, "There is no one like you.You protect the weak from the strong, The poor from the oppressor!"

Evil people testify against me and accuse me of crimes I know nothing about. They pay me back evil for good, and I sink in despair. But when they were sick , I dressed in mourning; I deprived myself of food; I prayed with my head bowed low as I would pray for a friend or a brother. I went about bent over in mourning, as one who mourns for his mother.

Be wise evil spirits are real

Order your More Than Conquerors Magazine now
Tel: 0208 694 9694

Order your More Than Conquerors Magazine now
Tel: 0208 694 9694

Be wise evil spirits are real

Books and tapes by Archbishop Gilbert Deya